COUNTRY
MUSIC STARS

Edited by Benjamin Howard Smith

Crescent Books

New York • Avenel, New Jersey

Introduction and Compilation
Copyright © 1994 by Starlog Communications International

First published in 1994 by Crescent Books
distributed by Random House Value Publishing, Inc.,
40 Engelhard Avenue, Avenel, New Jersey 07001

Random House
New York • Toronto • London • Sydney • Auckland

Manufactured in the United States

Library of Congress Cataloging-in-Publication Data
Country music stars / edited by Benjamin Howard Smith.
     p. cm.
   Includes index.
   ISBN 0-517-08930-0
   1. Country music—History and criticism. 2. Country musicians—
United States. I. Smith, Benjamin Howard.
ML3524.C77 1994
781.642'092'273—dc20   94-13633
                                                        CIP
                                                        MN

CONTENTS

GARTH BROOKS
COUNTRY'S NEW KING

It's funny how a chubby kid can just be having fun, and they call that entertainment," Garth Brooks said once upon winning the CMA Entertainer of the year award. In light of Garth Brooks selling over 30 million albums in the U.S. alone, such a comment could be taken as false modesty. But with Garth, you know that he means it, because his very real persona that comes through on all his records is what he's really about. He's just a regular guy for the most part, and he has many of the concerns that his fans have, like good times, good friends, and a safe home to return to at night.

In a music world seemingly overrun by Madonnas, Michael Jacksons and Guns 'N Roses, all in a tizzy over their own desperate sense of self importance, Garth Brooks is like a clean breath of fresh air. There isn't a hint of trendyness in his music, and he doesn't rely on an overblown image or media hype to reach his fans. But a down to earth image can't explain an artist's popularity. In fact, it's hard to explain Garth's phenomenal success in simple terms. Because no country artist has ever debuted an album atop the pop charts, as Garth has done more than once. And no country artist ever sold ten million records with a single album, as Garth did with his second effort, *No Fences*.

Perhaps part of the answer can be heard in the lead-off cut from his 3rd album *Ropin' The Wind,* "Against The Grain." "You can't follow like a bunch of sheep/You got to listen to your heart/Go bustin' in like old John Wayne/Sometimes you got to go against the grain," the song demands. And in an America that has become increasingly conformist, these words are going to strike a chord in those who want to cut their own path and think of themselves as individuals.

Many singers have repeated this idea, but the difference is that Brooks puts his money where his mouth is. He started as a country artist and he's still a country artist, despite the lure of the even greater commercial success he might find if he sold out to the trappings of pop stardom, namely trying to land singles

Garth Brooks' latest record, *In Pieces,* was not his first to debut at No. 1 on both the Country *and* Pop charts.

on the pop charts and releasing video after video in an effort to court the fickle teenage audience.

That's not Garth, though. With all his hits, he's never catered to the hot 100 or to top 40 radio stations. His record company likes this just fine. Why should they want to throw money all over the place for independent promotion when the records are selling anyway? But the video question is really the confounding part for record execs. "You can't have a hit without major video play!" they would all probably concur. But Garth's popularity has remained constant regardless of "Buzz Clips" and rapid fire editing.

"The Thunder Rolls" video stirred controversy throughout the country when it was banned by both CMT and TNN for its depiction of an abusive husband who also cheats on his wife and the further violence that occurs when the wife finally turns on him and shoots him dead. But the conservative music TV networks who rejected the clip were among the few that were offended by the video. Thousands of women's shelters across America used the video in group counseling sessions, publicly thanking Brooks for his courageous stand. His quadruple platinum home video project, which features performance and interview footage as well as his music videos, was released as well.

Apparently, someone wanted to see the video, probably because of the serious nature of the songs and their depiction. Garth maintains that he won't make a video unless he feels that it will add something to the song, and his visual work can be very inspiring. Garth even appears as the villain in "The Thunder Rolls" video, and ironically, the sleaziness he exudes is quite convincing.

The acting experience Garth gained during the filming of the video paid off when the singer was asked to guest star in NBC's hit comedy series, "Empty Nest." *TV Guide*'s Timothy Carlson noted: "Brooks showed comic prowess in rehearsals, quickly developing appro-

priate double takes—and perfectly replicating them." "That's a skill many film actors don't have, but stage actors do," said director Steve Zuckerman. "He sees the whole scene, not just his words." Maybe Garth has a future in film as a sideline.

But for the moment, Garth Brooks will most surely be known for his blockbuster albums. Garth writes most of the songs he records, and he has this to say of some of his standouts: " 'Burning Bridges' is what I was about when I was younger. Thanks to the Lord and my wife, I got past that stage. And 'Cold Shoulder' was an idea I got while I was driving to my wife's parents for Christmas, and saw an eighteen wheeler sitting beside the road. It occurred to me that he wasn't going to make it home for Christmas, hugging that old cold shoulder on the highway."

Another strong composition is so visual that it might be called an audio movie: "In Lonesome Dove," co-written with Cynthia Limbaugh. "I tried and tried to make another town's name work on that song," Garth admits. "Obviously the book and the film had already defined that name. But no other title worked as good, so I decided to leave it alone.

"If I'm driving down the road, and something comes on (the radio), and it makes me think, and it upsets me—that's good! If you're upset after a song, that's good. It's as good as crying after a song, or it's as good as changing your life after a song. As long as it brings an emotion, then you know you're living." Country music, according to Garth Brooks, is the only kind of music today that consistently has this kind of emotion.

Country music, he emphasized, "is a format that hangs on to the lyric, and I think the lyric is becoming everyday life. It's the 10 o'clock news put to music. And I think that people are looking for something to learn from."

Brooks deplores that so much of today's music "almost drops the lyric out of what they are trying to

"Country music is a lot more about everyday life now, than centrally focused on love— good or bad."

Since the birth of his daughter Taylor, Garth Brooks has become a road daddy, who takes his family with him when he tours.

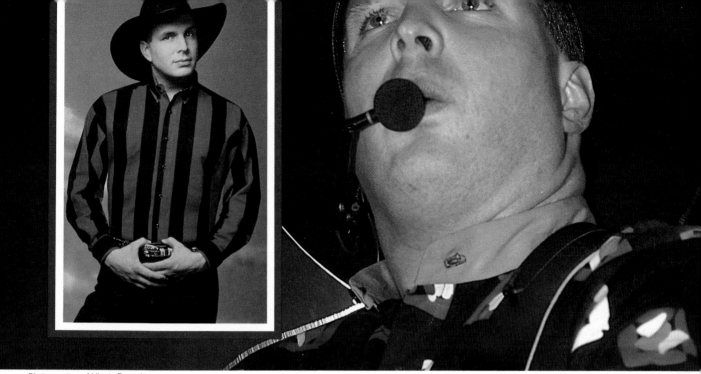

Garth likes to save the first two rows at his shows for people who got stuck in the back of the concert hall.

say," with some exceptions. "I found that country music was the format that was hanging on to that (lyrically). Sometimes the way other music is produced, or the way their music is influenced, it goes by so fast, or it's so drowned out that you cannot understand what they're saying. So that's why (I love) country music."

As for the popularity of today's country music, Garth acknowledged "I'm not sure the country music audience hasn't been this big in the past—just never recognized. The country music audience is a huge market to be faced, and I think they're getting the light shone on them that they deserved for several years. I think that is the reason that country music is being exposed now."

As for people who don't normally tune in country music, Brooks noted that there has been a big change in the past five or six years. "Country music is a lot more about everyday life now, than centrally focused on love—good or bad. Country music is alive and well, but it's also a very viable form of entertainment, and it's also a very alternative format to turn to if you're not particularly happy with the music that you're hearing somewhere else."

Country, he added, isn't just the "heartbroke kind of cheating songs," as was in the past. "I want people to take all the great things about country music they had 10 years ago, back to the legendary status of the Jones' and the Haggards—that strength. Hang on to that,

because that's still there."

The singer has always admitted that growing up in a small Oklahoma town, his idols were rock groups, such as Kiss, Queen and others. But he also noted that "Billy Joel is a huge influence on our music," as were James Taylor, Dan Fogelberg, Elton John, George Strait, Boston, George Jones, Kansas, Janis Joplin and Rita Coolidge—"All those people that I grew up listening to."

Garth Brooks has been nominated for numerous awards, and has won many of them, including best artist, best pop artist, ad infinitum. He has cut an album with Ray Charles on Quincy Jones' Qwest label, and critics acclaimed his acting performance on Kenny Rogers' Christmas TV special. But what really got Garth hopped up was winning video awards.

Finally, Garth stressed that "Music is a very, very powerful thing. Passion and emotion. So even though this thing (career) could end tomorrow—and I must live it like it might—I also have to rely on my first goal, and that is to consume that power, to try and emote people to do things that they wouldn't have done, to take people out on the edge that have been playing it safe. Because I think that when we all extend ourselves, only better things come.

"And that's what I do—or try to do." —*C.B. & F.B.*

BILLY RAY CYRUS
ACHY BREAKY HEART-THROB

Garth Brooks paved the way for country crooners to shoot straight to the top of the pops, and Billy Ray Cyrus wasted no time following suit. His debut album *Some Gave All* went platinum three days after its release and edged out big-leaguers U2, Def Leppard, and Mariah Carey for the No. 1 pop spot. His hit single "Achy Breaky Heart" spawned a dance craze, his follow-up album, *It Won't Be The Last,* went Top Ten and with his hot looks, Billy Ray has fast become the nation's latest heartthrob.

Cyrus inspires unbelievable amounts of adulation. Radio man Pat McCoy boldly asserts: "This guy is going to be the biggest thing in country music, and possibly pop music for that matter, since the King." Radio man Alan Rice says, "This churnin' urn of burnin' funk could ignite fires with wet wood." Other radio personalities rave: "It's like CMA meets GQ." Cyrus rocks as much as he twangs. He belongs to the new generation of country artists with crossover appeal—a group that includes Garth Brooks, k.d. lang, and Wynonna.

But this newcomer seems to be outpacing them all for the moment. Cyrus is holding up well under the pressure. He maintains that "no matter what happens—

all the money in the world, all the platinum albums—even if they were all gone tomorrow, it can never get better than what it is right now." Whenever he feels overwhelmed, he remembers his father's words: "Bo, know where you're going, always be aware of where you're at, and most of all, never forget where you come from." With such sudden fame, "I hope I can have the wisdom and intelligence to use it for something good and bow my head and thank the good Lord above."

Billy Ray keeps a more balanced perspective on himself than those around him. It's hard to believe that the quiet, polite man is the same as the one rockin' the house every night. "I definitely have two personalities. If I was laid back I would bore these people to tears." Nicknamed the "Cyrus Virus" and the "tennis shoe cowboy," Billy Ray is most often compared to the King himself. "Elvis has always been an influence but I don't consciously do anything to copy him. I admire the man and am learning a little bit of what he went through." Cyrus fan Becky Barrett says, "Now that I have seen Billy Ray, I have finally put Elvis to bed."

Cyrus began humbly enough in Flatwoods, Kentucky. He had never really thought about music as a career until he had a strange experience at age 20. He swears he heard a voice telling him to buy a guitar and start singing. Cyrus could not even imagine himself as a singer—he wanted to play professional baseball. "I wanted to grow up to be Johnny Bench. I was a really good catcher—that was my home behind the plate. In high school, I wouldn't even get up to dance at the school dances because I was nervous, and to think I might jump up in front of people and sing was ludicrous." But against all reason, he found himself buying a guitar and forming a band called Sly Dog. He decided to test out the vision the voice had laid out for him. He told himself he'd give music ten months—if he and his band didn't get a gig by then, he'd quit. Almost to the day of his self-imposed deadline, Sly Dog got its first gig in Ironton, Ohio.

Cyrus shifted around for a few years, selling Oldsmobiles and playing in California bands. He ended up in West Virginia and spent the next five years headlining at a local joint. Every spare second he got, he would drive to Nashville and literally go through the phone book to find someone who would listen to him. "In 1989, I made 42 trips and that's a six-hour drive each way. I was still playing five nights a week, and on my two days off, I'd go to Nashville, knock on doors, then drive back and get onstage."

Finally country star Del Reeves listened to him and not only cut one of Cyrus's songs, but introduced him to his former manager Jack McFadden. Not long after, the Mercury Records A&R team heard Billy Ray perform with Reba McEntire. Quite impressed with what they saw, Mercury soon handed Cyrus his first record deal. For a debut artist, Cyrus managed to exert a lot of

Billy Ray Mania first broke out after a performance in Tupelo, Mississippi, birthplace of Elvis Presley!

"I wouldn't even get up to dance at the school dances because I was nervous, and to think I might jump up in front of people and sing was ludicrous."

13

Billy Ray has said that despite the quick overturn rate in pop music, one thing is for sure, he'll die making music.

A chance meeting with a Vietnam vet profoundly changed Cyrus.

the time came, and performed it this past Memorial Day. But Kane is the one person Cyrus has yet to sing it to. "I've had the state police in three different states look for him, but we can't find him. I really wanted him to hear the song."

On "Wher'm I Gonna Live (When I Get Home)?" Cyrus gives half the writing credits to his ex-wife Cindy. He thanks her for kicking him out and giving him the inspiration for the song. In concert, Cyrus introduced Cindy to the crowd and then shocked her by saying, "So darling, since you was so sweet to set my stuff out on that cold rainy night, I dedicate this song to you." Cindy takes it in stride. "We're really better friends now than ever," she says, swearing that he is "the kindest person offstage, very different from his onstage person. He's very soft-spoken, the most polite man you would ever meet."

The soft-spoken man quickly becomes a wild man once on stage, especially when performing the much-hyped "Achy Breaky Heart." The song was canned by every record company until Mercury. According to Cyrus, "The first time I heard it, I immediately fell in love with it. It hit me like a hit record does." Mercury shrewdly promoted the single. Choreographer Melanie Greenwood was brought in to create the "Achy Breaky Dance," as well as an instructional video. Dance clubs across the country held contests and radio stations were besieged by requests for the song that had yet to be released. Mercury now holds the distinction of producing the first country dance created specifically for a country song. Mercury's Steve Miller says, "We felt that creating a new dance would highlight the uniqueness of the song and Billy Ray Cyrus." The video was shot near Cyrus's Kentucky home in an art deco theater. "I wanted to do my first video here with the folks who have believed in me and my music through the years. They've helped me get through some tough times and it's important to me that those people have an opportunity to share this exciting new experience with me."

This hot new artist, already enslaved to a grueling schedule of interviews, appearances, and performances, is discovering the hard work that goes into being a star, but he's determined to make his success a good example for others. "One thing I've studied hard

control over the album's production. He insisted on recording with his own band instead of studio musicians, and he penned six of the ten songs. The sound is straight from the heart. "I don't do anything matter-of-fact. Most of my songs come to me as fast as I can speak them. The songs on the album that I haven't written are all songs that I relate to. The very best description of my music is my life."

A chance meeting with a Vietnam vet profoundly changed Cyrus and gave him the title of the album. After relating the horrors of jungle warfare, vet Sandy Kane gave Cyrus his hat and asked him to deliver it to MIA/POW advocate Charlie Daniels. Before leaving, Kane turned to say: "Something tells me I should tell you this—in rehab camp they used to say all gave some, but some gave all." It struck Cyrus, and driving home, the lyrics came pouring out. "A lot of my songs come fast, but that one came as if it were inside the car with me." Cyrus quickly made a demo to give Charlie Daniels along with Kane's hat. Luckily, Daniels never used the song, and Cyrus put it on his own album when is successful people—Norman Vincent Peale. Thomas Edison. I hope that if my career goes the way I want it to, I can do something positive to show kids that it doesn't matter where you're born and what handicaps you're born with; you can be whatever you want to be." Cyrus adds truth to the saying that success does not come overnight, and he has been preparing for his for 12 years. And he seems to really love it. "The great thing is, I don't do this for money. One of the biggest philosophies of my life is, 'As ye sow, so shall ye reap.' Everything is a boomerang, and I'm sure I probably have some bad boomerangs coming back at me someday. But as often as I can intentionally throw out a good boomerang, I try to do it."

With the release of his second album, *It Won't Be The Last,* Cyrus repeated his debut's success. His follow-up effort is equal parts country and rock—true to his Led Zeppelin and George Jones roots. The album's themes of love and relationships appeal to his largely female following. His bluesy lyrics about heartbreak are mellow and dynamically contrast the more raucous guitar licks, especially in "Heart Of A Woman." His vocals are full of a sophomoric yearning.

"Words By Heart" is quite poignant, written by Reed Nielsen and Monty Powell, about finding an old goodbye letter in a jacket pocket. "There was no need to read. I knew just what it would say/I knew the words by heart, I know every line/From 'this ain't easy' to 'you'll get along just fine'/I know every comma, every question mark/No I don't have to look—I know the words by heart." "When I'm Gone" with its simple guitar strum and its gospel backup vocals by the Jordanaires, has a slow, seductive groove. The honky-tonk "Throwin' Stones" and "Ain't Your Dog No More" are the get-up-and-dance Achy Breaky wannabes of this album.

Cyrus is definitely contributing to country music's current popularity. His music is accessible to the general public, and his tight jeans and muscle t-shirts are driving women wild. Toronto editor Jim Baine says, "I think he's taking down the last barrier between country and rock. Garth Brooks broke it a bit but this guy takes it further." If Cyrus can survive the Achy Breaky craze, he can survive the trap of short-lived pop stardom. As long as he remains more man than marketed product, Billy Ray Cyrus will be gyrating on stage for many years to come.—K.F.

The title of BRC's first album, *Some Gave All* was inspired by a brief encounter Cyrus had with a Vietnam War veteran, Sandy Kane.

A recent poll showed that Billy Ray was one of the men that women fantasized about most often.

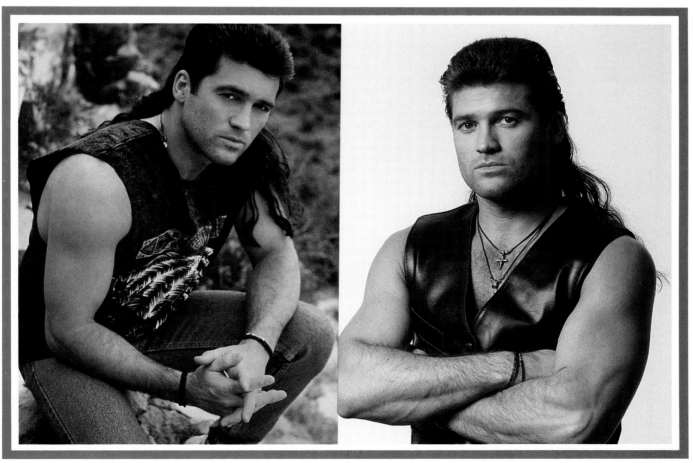

Lorrie Morgan has finally risen to the top despite years of hard work in obscurity and the death of her husband, Keith Whitley.

LORRIE MORGAN
PAID IN FULL!

L orrie Morgan is a classic case of someone who has paid her dues. Although her dad, George Morgan, was a longtime Opry star (his 1949 hit, "Candy Kisses," was major-major), she never found the easy entree most people assume comes with *that* territory.

Making her debut when a lot of us are still flipping baseball cards, she did in fact make a splash. "My little 13-year-old knees were absolutely knocking," she says, "but I saw Dad standing there just bawling, and those people gave me a standing ovation. I thought, 'This is what I'm doing the rest of my life.' I thought it was going to be easy. Little did I know."

Lorrie toured with her father until his death in 1975, then did a number of years of road dates on her own, a period that had more than its share of hard times. "I drove thousands of miles with just me and my mom or me and one musician. There were times I couldn't get through a show without literally crying because the band was so bad. But I think there's a reason why I did all that, and it makes me appreciate what a good band I have now, and what good management and label support. It's hard to appreciate the good things you have unless you've been without them."

Things didn't start to progress until she began writing songs herself. "I started writing and got on as a writer at Acuff-Rose," she recalls. "From there, I went on to be their receptionist. I did a lot of demo sessions during my lunch hour and after work. Any time they asked me to do a demo, I would do it, and finally I got signed to Hickory Records, which was owned by Acuff-Rose."

"There were times I couldn't get through a show without crying because the band was so bad."

Lorrie's father, country singer George Morgan, is best remembered for his 1949 hit, "Candy Kisses."

Photo by John Lee

"It's hard to appreciate good things unless you've been without them."

But full-fledged success was still elusive. She had a few minor singles and a 'Best New Female Artist' nomination from the A.C.M., but the road was taking its toll. She looked for a better deal, but none was in the offing. "I thought to myself, 'This is the last time I'm going to try this.' I was working the road, doing the Nashville Network, playing the Grand Ole Opry, and still doing some demo sessions and writing, and I knew there would be one more opportunity for a record label to come my way. Had RCA not accepted that session, I wasn't sure what I was going to do, but I wasn't going to get turned down any more."

Even then, her climb to the top was a tough one, combining career demands with single motherhood following the death of her husband Keith Whitley. But with her third album, *Watch Me* selling well for over a year and her two previous ones, *Leave The Light On* and *Something In Red* firmly ensconced in the charts, Lorrie finally has a bit of breathing room.

"I don't think it's so much what you sing, it's how you project it, how you make the audience understand the way you feel it," Lorrie Morgan says of the emotive style that has made her famous. "That's why every song I put in my show has a meaning for me. There's always a reason why it's there."

"When I go into one of my songs and hear the applause, it's a good feeling. This is what I've worked for, to be recognized and to be respected."—C.B.

Photo by John Lee

ALAN JACKSON

SAGE OF THE REAL WORLD

"Music was always in my life, but I didn't grow up thinking I'd ever get to do it professionally."
—Alan Jackson

Alan Jackson has risen to the top of the country music world. His finely-tuned songwriting talents, poignant lyrics, and emotional voice have landed him a series of gold and platinum albums, as well as a string of magazine covers. He charted four consecutive Number One singles from his debut album, *Here In The Real World:* the title track, "Wanted," "Chasin' That Neon Rainbow," and "I'd Love You All Over Again." On June 7, 1991, he became the 68th inductee to the Grand Ole Opry, and he has accumulated a vast collection of music awards. His second album, *Don't Rock The Jukebox,* was certified gold only four weeks after its release, and his latest record, *A Lot About Livin'* (*And A Little 'Bout Love*), contained the CMA winning song and video "Chattahoochee."

Growing up in Newnan, Georgia—a town south of Atlanta with a population of about 30,000, he was the youngest and only boy in a large family. His father worked as a mechanic, an influence that follows Alan Jackson to this day. He began working in a shoe store when he was twelve, later held a job in a furniture store, and at fifteen, bought his first car, a 1955 Thunderbird. Two years later, he met his future wife, Denise. At twenty, they married, and Jackson worked a variety of jobs over the years: automobile sales,

Alan Jackson's song "Chattahoochee" was named 1993's Song and Video of the Year by the CMA.

Photo courtesy of Arista Records

19

Photo courtesy of Arista Records

"Whatever I was doing for a living, I'd just get tired of it. Music's the only thing I kept coming back to."

rebuilding houses. But, he admits, "Whatever I was doing for a living, I'd just get tired of it. Music's the only thing I kept coming back to, but I didn't, at first, think that was any big deal. Growing up, we didn't even listen much to the radio, except maybe some gospel. And we watched *Hee Haw*.

"We loved music, and we all sang . . . at church, around the house, in the car. Then, during high school, I did some singing with a duet partner, just local performances. But I was about twenty years old before I went to my first concert or ever saw any of the big country acts. About that time, I start having this two-year burnout on my jobs, but I still didn't think of seriously pursuing music.

"One thing that probably got me going was that one of my best friends had started flying these little planes in high school, and said he was going to be an airline pilot. Well, that was about as far out of reach as being a singer, but by the time I was twenty-three, he was doing it. That's when I told myself I really ought to be

doing the music thing. It was all I'd ever really wanted to do, and I'd never really taken the chance on it. So I told my wife I was going to sell the house and move us to Nashville."

What followed has probably become the most often-told story about Alan Jackson's career. His wife was working as a flight attendant while he continued a summer job at a Newnan marina. The house having already been sold, he lived in a trailer and spent his free moments concentrating on songwriting. He picks up the story: "I had already planned to go to Nashville, but I'd never been there before, and I had no earthly idea what a publisher was, or a producer, or anything. Then one day, Denise was waiting on a flight in Atlanta and saw Glen Campbell sitting there with his band. Now we'd never been around stars, but she went right up to Glen and said, 'Excuse me, my husband's about to move to Nashville to be a singer and songwriter. What does he need to do?' And Glen gave her a card with the name and address of his office in Nashville on it."

As a result, Jackson landed a publishing deal, and shortly after, assembled a band, found a manager, and became the first country signing to Arista Records. Upon release of his debut, he immediately shot to the top, and found himself endlessly on the road. Between writing, recording, and touring, he also found time for charitable efforts, including Farm Aid 1990, the Arista Records 15th Anniversary Concert benefitting the AIDS crisis, and a variety of appearances to assist the homeless and needy children. Touring with Randy Travis opened up another avenue. The two discovered a natural flair for teamwork, and have penned quite a few excellent songs together. In the rare moments he has to himself, Jackson returns to his first love: repairing and restoring automobiles. Having grown up around engines, he now dedicates himself to fixing cars, boats, motorcycles . . . as he puts it, "Anything except air planes." He recently acquired and restored a 1958 Harley-Davidson, his first vintage model, and is working on a boat collection. He quips, "You might think this is crazy, but it's the truth: I have owned and sold, personally, at least 300 boats, cars, and motorcycles since the age of fifteen. By now, my wife's used to it. I could drive up in practically anything, and she wouldn't bat an eye."

He doesn't take his success lightly, nor has he forgotten the hard times when there was no material wealth around him. "It seems everyone wants to come up with a great story about music in my background, but it's not like I grew up with a guitar in my hands," he explains. "Music was always in my life, but I didn't grow up thinking I'd ever get to do it professionally. In a small town, you have to understand, you go to school, then you go to college, then you get married, and you have a kid or two. You've got this pattern that you just kind of follow, and everybody does the same thing. And something like singing in Nashville, or having a record out, that was just another world. A dream. Something you couldn't really achieve."

Against all odds, however, he pursued his rainbow and is now an inspiration to other artists whose sights are set on a recording contract. If he could give them any advice, or share his most valuable learning experience with them, it would probably go something like this: "The writing has helped my career more than anything. I've been holding on to all my songs, and that's kind of taking a chance, I know. If you've got a song that somebody wants to record, and you want to wait, and hope you can do it yourself—well, that's a hard decision to make. But when I came here, I wanted to carry on the tradition of real Country music. And I'd like to stay that way. It isn't easy to keep your feet on the ground up here. You get separated from working people, from real life. Now you go sit out in the audiences at *The Nashville Network,* or at Fan Fair, and you know who the real fans are, the ones who listen to country radio. They're just good people who love music, and I hope what I'm trying to do is what they want."—*E.H.*

Alan Jackson's big break came when his wife, Denise, sought the advice of Glen Campbell as he was waiting for a flight at the airport where she worked.

Jackson says that he has owned or sold over 300 boats, cars and motorcycles in his lifetime.

VINCE GILL

HIS SONGS ARE FULL OF GOLD

Vince grew up in Oklahoma, playing bluegrass music.

Vince Gill's 1993 album, *I Still Believe In You*, swept most of the honors in 1993 CMA Awards.

The single moment that pinpoints the arrival of Vince Gill came on the night of the Country Music Association's annual awards show in October of 1990. He leaned into the wailing high notes of "When I Call Your Name," electrifying not only a Grand Ole Opry House full of his peers, but a national TV audience as well. It seemed that the entire world of country music stopped for a moment. Then there was a standing ovation, and from that point on, the world turned his way. Vince Gill had truly arrived.

Even before his arrival in Nashville in 1984, Vince was well-known as one of the most talented individuals in the music business. Not raw talent, either, but refined, blessed with a pure tenor voice and a riveting, pitch-perfect delivery. He's a studio-quality guitarist whose style is fiery but still tasteful. When he's not working on his own records he's in great demand as a musician and singer for other artists' projects. His songs are passionate and heartfelt and could be hits for anyone.

Vince grew up in Oklahoma, playing bluegrass music. His first instruments were a four-string tenor guitar and his dad's banjo. In high school, he made a name for himself in bluegrass circles as a member of Mountain Smoke, whose credits included opening a concert for the pop group Pure Prairie League, whose biggest hit

at the time was "Amie." The summer after high school, Gill was seriously considering a career as a professional golfer when a call came from Louisville, Kentucky. He threw all his belongings into his van and went off to join the Bluegrass Alliance, a progressive bluegrass group whose members at that time included Sam Bush and Dan Crary.

After a year, Gill left for Los Angeles for a two-year stint with the group Sundance, led by bluegrass fiddler Byron Berline. He joined Pure Prairie League almost by accident. He had gone along with a friend to an audition just to see if they remembered him from his Mountain Smoke days. They not only remembered him, they offered him a job. He recorded three albums with the group and put them back on the charts with his lead vocal on "Let Me Love You Tonight."

When I Call Your Name was the album that brought Vince's many talents to the attention of the public. By the summer of 1990, the title cut had hit #1, and Gill

The first sign that Gill had come into his own was the standing ovation he received when he played at the Grand Ole Opry in 1990.

was packing in the crowds at his live shows.

Having proven his versatility with *When I Call Your Name*, Gill settled into a more clearly defined country style in writing songs for *Pocket Full Of Gold*. "The first album hit a lot of different pockets musically," he explained. "On *Pocket Full Of Gold* I felt more at ease singing and recording songs that were a little more straight-ahead country. That album feels very relaxed and very comfortable to me. It feels good."

Vince Gill's third MCA album, *I Still Believe In You*, finds each element of his artistry in top form. His vocal performances are riveting, pitch-perfect, at times making accompaniment seem almost unnecessary. His lead guitar parts are not only technically impressive, they are an integral part of the songs. The songs themselves—all written by Gill—are heartfelt and universally appealing.

Many of Gill's songs—particularly those about sadness or sinful behavior—represent a break from the country tradition in that they were *not* inspired by Gill's personal life. If he focuses only on himself, he explains, "I find that the songs get too one dimensional and too personal. People don't want to hear just about me when I write songs. They want to have lyrics that pertain to how they feel and what goes on in their life. Obviously I try to appeal in an ambiguous kind of way where everybody can pull something out of it. I never intended for 'When I Call Your Name' to mean anything about death or the loss of someone. I've had a ton of people tell me that song meant that to them. It makes perfectly good sense when you think about it in that way. A guy put some of the lyrics of 'Look At Us' on his tombstone. When he passed away his family did it because he loved the song so much. I try not to be self-indulgent in my work."

Gill said he felt more at ease, more relaxed in preparing for *I Still Believe In You* than with any of his previous albums. The only goal was to combine all the best elements of the previous two albums. *"When I Call Your Name* was very diverse," he explains. "We tried a little bit of everything, and threw it up against the wall to see what sticks. On *Pocket Full Of Gold*, we narrowed it down, maybe a little too far. With this album, we tried to get the best of *When I Call Your Name* and the best of *Pocket Full Of Gold*."

The result of his efforts, *I Still Believe In You*, covers a wide range of musical styles and emotional situations, all brought into focus to create a powerful artistic statement by one of the most talented artists in country music today—Vince Gill.

Photo by Victoria Pearson/courtesy of MCA Records

Vince Gill is one of the few country frontmen who are as respected as instrumentalists as they are as singers.

Many of Gill's songs represent a break from the country tradition.

Photo by Victoria Pearson/courtesy of MCA Records

In 1991, Black married actress Lisa Hartman, and he says the marriage has strengthened and transformed him.

"I'm an observer, somebody who's trying to sum things up."

CLINT BLACK

NO TIME TO KILL!

Listening to Clint Black's *Killin' Time* and *Put Yourself In My Shoes,* it's impossible not to wonder how much Black resembles the subjects of his songs.

"I'm a lot like the guy in 'A Better Man,' and 'Walkin' Away,' " Black admits. "And at one time I was like the guy in 'Nobody's Home.' I am really more of an observer, somebody who's just trying to sum things up and say something in an enjoyable and musical way, something that people can relate to. My songs come out of my own life experiences, but a great deal more out of other people's."

The youngest of four musical sons, Clint took full advantage of his brothers' performing experience. He grew up in Houston, performing with his brothers at the family's backyard barbeques. "They'd go all night long, and when my brothers took a break I'd sit on a stool in the middle of the yard and keep going. And I'd do the same thing at Bear Creek Park, just west of Houston, where I'd go from picnic table to picnic table singing to anybody who'd listen, anybody who looked like they wanted to hear a song or two. I just loved singing for people and I decided then that I would travel the world over to do it."

By the end of high school, Clint knew he wanted to do nothing but perform. He soon discovered, however, that making a living doing it was another matter. He survived those beginning years by working in construction as a "rod buster" (iron worker), as a bait cutter and as a fishing guide—but always performing his music on the side somewhere.

Through a family friend, he won his first solo gig in 1981 at Houston's Benton Springs Club. "I was singing a lot of folk and Texas 'cosmic cowboy' stuff," he relates about those days. What followed was six years of playing the Houston club circuit. Not only did he develop his performing skills, but he started writing songs about his experiences.

True to his Texas lineage, Black started out playing "cosmic cowboy" songs in the vein of Rocky Erickson.

At one of the club dates, Clint met and began collaborating with Hayden Nicholas. Hayden had an eight-track studio in his home, so they were able to record their songs.

Finally, Clint was able to get a tape to Bill Ham—Houston based manager/producer of ZZ Top. After one listen, Ham knew he had found the country act he had been seeking and summoned Clint for a meeting. Clint arrived at the offices of Lone Wolf Management the next morning with guitar in hand, and proceeded to perform for Ham as if it were back in the early days of playing in the parks. After that impromptu performance, they shook hands, and three weeks later Clint found himself sitting in the Nashville office of the head of RCA's country division.

Killin' Time, Clint's debut album, went Double Platinum, was named Album of the Year by the Academy of Country Music and resulted in his being named not only Best New Vocalist, but Best Male Vocalist!

Clint is recognized as the total professional. "This is my job," he says. "I've concentrated on it since I was 15. I've known I wanted to write and perform and I've given that my attention and focus, just as a lawyer would the law books."

Photo courtesy of RCA Records

Most people would be swept away by the details of constant touring and recording, but Black thrives on it. "I love being systematic," he says. "I fight every day to keep the system in line. I'm a planner. I like to see that everybody (around me) is thinking two years ahead. I want to plan my next tour now."

Part of Black's system—and one that has served him well in *No Time To Kill*—his aptly titled third album is setting aside a specific period to write instead of trying to squeeze the time in on the road. "If a song happens on the road," he says, "that's great. But I don't keep it in the back of my mind that I need to be writing when I really should be concentrating on something else. When I come off the road, I go on a combination vacation and writing session. I figure there's 24 hours in the day, so I need eight to sleep, eight to write, and eight for some really great distractions. If I look at it that way, writing an album doesn't seem overwhelming. It seems real possible."

In 1991, Black married actress Lisa Hartman. The marriage, he says, has strengthened and transformed him into "something better than I was." He pays his wife tribute on the eloquent and heart-felt song "Half The Man." "I don't think this song spells it all out," he observes. "I don't think I could write a song that would really live up to my feelings . . . but it's a start."

Because Black's writing and performances are so strong and varied on *No Time To Kill,* it is impossible to cite any one or two as representative. He explores over-intellectualizing love in "Thinkin' Again," obsession with love in "A Good Run Of Bad Luck" and the supportiveness of love in "Back To Back." In "State Of Mind," he marvels at the mood-altering power of music; and in "Happiness Alone" (which he co-wrote with Jimmy Buffett) he draws the truly wry conclusion that having a good time isn't enough for emotional survival.

To assist him in recording *No Time To Kill,* Black turned into a couple of his musical idols, Kenny Loggins and Timothy B. Schmitt. Loggins provides background vocals on the title cut and "Tuckered Out." Schmitt also sings background on these two songs, as well as on "State Of Mind," "Half The Man" and "Happiness Alone." Says Black, "A lot of times, you admire artists and the nostalgia for their music turns out to be greater than the experience of working with them. In this case, the experience was even greater than the nostalgia—and the nostalgia was great."

As with all his previous albums, Black co-produced *No Time To Kill* with James Stroud. He says that writing and recording an album is such an intense experience for him that it's impossible to stand outside the process: "I make these records and I lose my objectivity. All I can do is see how they hit everybody else."—*C.B.*

Clint Black was discovered by ZZ Top manager Bill Hamm, who had been looking for a country singer with a brave new sound.

While recording *No Time To Kill,* Clint Black recruited two of his musical idols, Kenny Loggins and Timothy B. Schmitt.

REBA McENTIRE
THE QUEEN OF COUNTRY!

People who don't know country music that well often complain that there are too many sad songs. But Reba McEntire feels that's one of the positive sides of the music. As for the type of country music songs that women are singing these days, Reba explains "Women in country music do sing about the bad side of life. And the way I handle that situation is that if I can sing about wife abuse, child abuse—anything like that, then hopefully, someone in that situation will be able to talk about it—will have the strength to come out and talk about it, and fix their situation."

In fact, she says, "That's country music. That's reality. That's everyday life. And that's what country music is noted for."

Reba McEntire's album, *For My Broken Heart*, offers a positive perspective. Certainly it is filled with sad songs, an avenue Reba has explored and effectively delivered before. But, as Reba said, "For me, singing sad songs often has a way of healing a situation. It gets the hurt out in the open—into the light, out of the darkness. I hope this album heals all our broken hearts."

That album came on the heels of her platinum release, *Rumor Has It. For My Broken Heart* was a

With movies, records and books in the works,
Reba McEntire has become country's first
renaissance woman.

powerfully emotional album, a reflection of what the artist herself had been going through since the tragic loss of seven band members and her tour manager earlier that year. As always, McEntire was meticulous in her song selection, choosing songs that are thought provoking and precise in their message.

For My Broken Heart is a palette of emotional colors, from the heart breaking title track, which deals with the realization that life does go on despite a broken relationship, to the poignant "The Greatest Man I Never Knew." Reba has never been an artist to shun emotionally loaded issues. She tackled the subject of wife abuse eloquently in 1987's "The Stairs," and the plight of illegal aliens in "Just Across the Rio Grande," also from the album *The Last One To Know.* Then, she addresses the issue of mercy killing in the song "Bobby."

"All Dressed Up (With Nowhere To Go)" could be one of the saddest songs the artist has ever recorded. It is a reminder that loneliness is, perhaps, the biggest problem the elderly face. The collection closes with "If I Had Only Known," a song dedicated to the memories of Reba's eight friends.

The honesty Reba puts into each and every performance has long been the attribute fans and critics have singled out and praised. Red Steagall saw it when he heard a nineteen year old Reba perform the National Anthem at the National Finals Rodeo in Oklahoma City in 1974.

Early in 1990, Reba added a new dimension to her entertainer acumen when she appeared in the sci-fi thriller *Tremors.* Reba the singer found a whole new audience as Reba the actress. Critics praised her portrayal of Heather Gummer, a survivalist who gamely puts up with her husband's fascination with army issue weapons, and wields a pretty mean shotgun herself.

The singer admits "I always wanted to get into movies. But leaving my music career is not in my plans. I love to tour. I love the aspect of being on stage and performing live. Doing a movie is totally different from anything involved in music, because you get a second or third chance." But, she adds, "doing the movie was the hardest work I've ever done because it was a lot of early hours, and a lot of late hours. But it was a big thrill to do it. I'd like to do more in the future, if possible." Reba has received numerous movie offers, but insists that films are much harder than music.

"Acting," she points out, however, "is very easy for me. I act on stage every night, because I have theme songs. I have story songs that I play that character of that song each and every night. Acting for me is fun. I thoroughly enjoy it."

Photo by Michael Benabib

"I always wanted to get into movies. But leaving my music career is not in my plans."

One way that Reba McEntire dealt with the tragic, accidental deaths of eight members of her band and road crew was by making the album *For My Broken Heart*.

Acting comes easily to Reba, she says, because she's up on stage performing nearly every night as it is.

Look for Reba's appearance in the upcoming Rob Reiner film, *North*.

Growing up, Reba was a big fan of TV westerns, she admits. "Barbara Stanwyck was my favorite actress in *The Big Valley*. Some of my other heroes were Clint Walker, Chuck Connors and Johnny Crawford in *The Rifleman*. But I don't believe that I'd be interested right now in a weekly TV series."

Whatever her pursuit, Reba gives it her all. She credits parents Jacqueline and Clark McEntire with instilling in her that Oklahoma no-nonsense sensibility. And she has found another balance in her life thanks to son Shelby, born February, 1990. According to Reba, his birth gave her a whole new perspective.

"Family is my main priority. Shelby, my son, is three years old. Need I say more? He's quite a character and he keeps us thoroughly entertained, he's the entertainer of the family. I love what I do and I'm very lucky because my husband, Narvel Blackstock, is my manager and so Shelby gets to go with us quite a bit. He always knows the songlist and he has his favorite songs. When he's not out watching Mama perform, he's in back playing with the crew or talking on CB radios in the trucks and buses. So he's got everybody pretty much under control."

The Spring of '94 is going to be very busy for Reba as well. "I have an autobiography that's going to be out at that time. I feel like I've been on the analyst's couch for the last 2 or 3 weeks, diving into a lot of my past. One of the funny things is when you recount the past in terms of your brothers and sisters, when the interviewer goes and interviews them, they get a totally different outlook. But of course, I'm right because it's my book (laughs)! It's going to be from birth to the present. It's tough. We write it all down and then say, 'so you really want to put that in?' And then say, 'well, let me sleep on it for a little bit.' I don't want to tell all my deep, dark secrets. But it's kind of like, 'is my life that eventful? Is it going to be interesting?' Why would anybody want to write a book about me? But there are already two unauthorized biographies out and they were pretty funny. So this one's coming out with me telling the story. There will be some stuff in there that I haven't talked about in interviews. I've always been a great collector of memories and bits and pieces of my family history. It's very exciting to me to have the opportunity to reminisce about my childhood and all the memories that have shaped my life and career. There have been devastating tragedies and record breaking triumphs, a lot of joy and some sadness, but that's my life. I intend for this to be a very honest look at my life."

Ultimately, the Queen of Country feels that variety is the spice of life. "I love to record, and do tours, photo sessions. It breaks up doing just one thing all the time," says Reba McEntire. "We're very fortunate that we get to do that. We love what we do, and it's the variety of things that we can do that makes it fun."

—*C.B. & F.B.*

34

Among George Strait's greatest honors is his American Vocation Success Award, presented to him by former President George Bush.

Photo by Ron Phillips

George Strait is an avid roper and remains an active member of the Professional Rodeo Cowboys Association.

Photo courtesy of Warner Bros

GEORGE STRAIT
MOVE OVER, ELVIS!

He picked up a Hank Williams songbook and taught himself to play guitar.

As country music's recognized king of swing, George Strait has proven to be a real trendsetter, as well as a favorite among country audiences. With his white hat, neatly pressed shirt, and creased, never-faded jeans, he presents a clean-cut, healthy image that any fan can relate to and appreciate. It is this very look that landed him a spot in *People* Magazine's "50 Most Beautiful People In The World" special issue. But this kind of recognition is something that George Strait has learned to take with a grain of salt. He knows that what really counts is not swooning females or fashionable photo shoots. The key to his success is a fine ear for selecting quality songs to record, and the smooth-as-silk voice with which he delivers the material.

He was born in Pearsall, Texas, the son of a rancher and a school teacher. After high school, he married his long-time sweetheart, Norma, and began attending classes at Southwest Texas State University in San Marcos. Eventually, he joined the army, a step that would prove crucial to his future. While stationed in Hawaii, he picked up a Hank Williams songbook and taught himself to play guitar. A quick learner, he landed a slot in a country band that the base commander assembled. Strait soon discovered a fondness for the music of Merle Haggard, George Jones, and in particular, the original swing king, Bob Wills.

When he returned to Texas, Strait went back to school to finish studies and achieve a degree in agricultural education. However, he soon shelved the diploma and went back to the guitar, forming the Ace In The Hole band in 1975. The unit, with only one personnel change, remains intact, having survived years of grueling work across the Texas honky-tonks, dance halls, and assorted rough spots.

In a familiar story that many artists can tell, Strait spent five years playing bars while every record company repeatedly turned him down. He was about to give up music once and for all when a club owner made the right moves and helped him land a deal with MCA. It was certainly no error on the label's behalf. In the following ten years, Strait went on to chart 22 Number One singles, certify four platinum and ten gold albums, a double-platinum home video, and an endless string of sold out dates. He has broken attendance records set by Elvis Presley, and was presented with the American Vocation Success Award by President George Bush for his active role in vocational and technical education. He is country music's most successful live act, and ranks among the top 15 concert draws in any genre.

George Strait has always been known for his low-key, unassuming attitude. It was kind of surprising when he took the Country Music Association's "Entertainer of the Year" award for both 1989 and '90 after Hank Williams Jr., a much flashier star, controlled it in '87 and '88. But almost as quickly, Strait's reign at the top ended as the public turned its attention towards newcomers like Clint Black and Garth Brooks.

Then came a blow that nobody expected. In 1992, Strait wasn't even on the ballot. For the first time in years, he chose to watch the show on television at his home in Texas instead of attending, the snub was so great. There was even talk that the man who had knocked out over two dozen hits since his auspicious debut in 1981 with "Unwound" had seen his better days. But George wasn't looking at it that way.

"I hear this a lot. 'Well, you've accomplished all you can accomplish in country music.' I don't feel that way. I'm not through, and I think I've got a lot more to go," he told the Orange County Register late last year. His words proved to be prophetic. Since that time, he has returned to his previous level of success by starring in *Pure Country,* a movie that was tailor-made for his true-to-life, down-home personality. And the soundtrack album of the same name restored him to the top of the charts, as well.

In *Pure Country,* Strait plays a country star whose huge success forces him to wrestle with two divergent worlds: The simplicity of his roots and the glittery fast lane where his career has led him. Disillusioned, he returns to the rural life that inspired his music, falls in love with the headstrong Harley Tucker (played by Isabel Glasser), and finds a way to bring the two sides of his life together into a newly fulfilling whole.

Screen veteran Leslie Ann Warren starred opposite Strait, playing his zealously protective manager, Lula Rogers. Asked how he felt about making his acting debut, George replied that it took some getting used to. "I was really, really nervous. I didn't know how I would do. I never had taken any acting lessons. But I got in there and started rehearsing with her and shoot, I just relaxed, and we did it."

Strait says that he would like to make another movie, but for now, he's concentrating on regaining the stature he once held in the music biz. "I'd like to win 'Entertainer of the Year' again," he says. But don't expect him to change his style to win more fans anytime soon. "If people like country music," he declares, "let's keep playing country music. Don't change just to get a bigger audience."

With the release of another Greatest Hits collection, *Ten Strait Hits,* George Strait has once again encapsulated a period in his highly successful career. The close of that chapter, however, simply indicates the beginning of a new one, no doubt to be filled with more great music and concerts.—*E.H. & C.B.*

George Strait has broken attendance records set by Elvis Presley.

Photo by John Lee

36

DWIGHT YOAKAM
THOUGHTFUL HONKY-TONKER

His songs strike a raw nerve.

Dwight Yoakam generated a lot of interest in the rock press when he burst on the scene in 1986 with his first album, *Guitars, Cadillacs, Etc.,* and his music was erroneously called cow-punk. But the fact is, Dwight's sound draws from the roots of rock, namely western swing and R&B, and the skill and refinement with which he writes and records are anything but punk.

He does, however, strike a raw nerve with a lot of his songs, such as "It Won't Hurt" and "The Heart That You Own," and his arrangements pack a lot of punch. But who ever said that country can't rock?

Country music sure is booming.

Maybe it's not a boom but just a buoyancy during a recessionary time. But also I think that there's a certain level of success that's happening, Garth is certainly an example of that, where there are multi-platinum albums occurring almost simultaneously. That has never before happened in country music. I would say that the central and key factor in that is the advent of the Nashville Network and Country Music Television. TV is an impact medium. It sells everything from encyclopedias to dog collars. "Maybe America wants to get back to all these rural, basic values that are so instinctive and all . . ." that's romanticizing it. Come on. It's 1992.

How do you go about writing your songs?

Solitude first, and I try to write in a composite nature. My songs are generally a composite of emotions as opposed to a singular incident triggering the compulsion to write a song. Hopefully that talks to a more universal sense in all of us. For instance, take the *Buenas Noches* title track, "Red Dresses." I never went with a gun to the motel to kill somebody. It's an extension of an emotion that I had in maybe a couple of places in my life. It's also an extension of an emotion that's just called betrayal, generally. And that starts in childhood the first time your parents embarrass you or chastise you in public. You have this overwhelming sense of betrayal. I think that's a universal experience.

Dwight with longtime collaborator
and guitarist Pete Anderson.

Photo by John Lee

But your songs usually sound focused on a specific event.

I don't ever limit myself. It's kind of a philosophy that I affectionately refer to as momentary absolutism.

That's pretty heavy.

But it gives you all the latitude that you need. Momentary absolutism means that I'm completely a prisoner to the rigidity of the moment. But it's only rigid for that moment. It's absolutely, emphatically that way forever until it's not. It's an oxymoronic philosophy, but it's an oxymoronic world. Little Walter said it's a crazy mixed up world (laughs)!

What were your early years like?

I grew up, kinda obviously by the way this conversation is going, off of my own thoughts. And a by-product of our very pitiful public education system, but fortunate enough to have bumped into a few beacons on that dark path. A history teacher at one point when I was about thirteen, and a theatre coach and a band director in high school.

Did you ever feel like you were lost?

I never felt lost, but I sometimes felt abandoned.

Sometimes people label your music as being more rock than country.

What's country? What we're doing is sometimes a throwback to a more raw (approach). Ricky Skaggs first did it back in '81. Part of our approach has to do with us

being Californians. Go back and listen to Merle Haggard and Buck Owens stuff in the early '60's.

What's it like working with your collaborator, Pete Anderson?

We have a terrific rapport. It's great. We almost have a kind of sibling relationship, like we're brothers. Probably it's because neither of us have anything to gain from each other except what the other brought to that relationship. It's a mutually benefitting relationship. He and I are both very fortunate to have made each other's acquaintance.

What are some of your interests outside of music?

I love films and I'm trying to become a somewhat educated student of film. I was involved in theatre in my late teens and early twenties and I'd like to pursue that again. Outside of that, horses. I'm breeding some horses, having some fun with that. And I'm a perpetual student pilot.

Did you ever have any tough times before you made it?

Yeah! Like I was twenty-eight or twenty-nine years old before I finally signed a record deal. I drove an air freight truck around trying to eke out an existence.

What did you say to yourself to keep yourself going?

I'm right, they're wrong.

ight's latest record is *This Time*, featuring the hit "A Thousand Miles
m Nowhere."

"I never felt lost, but I sometimes felt abandoned."

Dwight Yoakam was among the first country artists who was as popular with the leather jacketed rockers as he was with good country folk.

WYNONNA
AND THEN THERE WAS ONE

Wynonna Judd was born in 1964 in Ashland, Kentucky. She moved to California at the age of four, but came back to Kentucky at ten. "That was when I discovered music," she recalled. "My influences—I thank God for this now—were the records from the old record shops, the used bins. Bluegrass was my first influence, the mountain harmonies, the mountain soul of Hazel and Alice, the harmonies of the family from the Delmore Brothers, the Stalney Brothers and the Louvin Brothers. And then I started listening to Bonnie Raitt. She's been one of the biggest influences on my vocal style."

By the time she became a teenager, Wynonna was completely wrapped up in music. "I didn't have a TV or telephone or Nintendo to occupy my time, so I had to play guitar to keep busy," she said. "I became so involved in music that I was way out in left field. I didn't go to dances, I didn't date. I didn't discover boys until I was 18 or 19."

She moved with her mother to Franklin, TN, near Nashville, at the age of 15. Her mother encouraged her music, but she also began to worry. "I became wrapped up in my own private world," Wynonna said. "I wanted to be in music more than anything in the whole world, but I had never been part of a band, never played anywhere. Every parent probably worries about their kids, but instead of worrying about me going out and drinking and driving, Mom was worried about me getting out of the house and getting a real job. She'd give me the classified ads to look for work, and she'd come home and the funnies would be covering it up."

The next eight years became life in a fishbowl. First

Wynonna and her mother, Naomi, in the Judd days. Despite rumors to the contrary, Wynonna says she and her mother have always been good friends.

The "Black & Wy" tour featured
Wynonna and Clint Black.

Wynonna's two solo albums were
produced by Tony Brown, known to
some as the "producer of the
decade."

came the famous live audition in RCA label head Joe
Galante's office backed only by Wynonna's guitar, then
the first show, playing to an audience of 10,000 people
opening for the Statler Brothers in 1984. The hits
started and kept coming.

The Judds' career came to an end when Naomi
announced plans to retire, due to chronic hepatitis.
Musically as well as emotionally, Wynonna had to face
the world alone. "I was 27 and I felt like I was leaving
home for the first time."

Wynonna's first album was a complete new beginning, with a new producer and new studio band. She
had never worked with Tony Brown before, but he was
hardly a stranger, having been at RCA when the Judds
performed their office audition. "I chose Tony not
because he was producer of the decade—which is

great—but because I wanted someone I knew,"
Wynonna said. "I'm a heart person. I know they say you
can't mix business with pleasure but life is too short to
work with people that you don't know or like.

"With the first album, I felt devastated. I had to get
up in the morning and go, 'Wynonna, I am, I can, I will.'
I had to talk to myself, have a lot of meetings with
myself. With the second album, I felt energized and
excited. The first album was 'I'm moving away from
home but I'm still going back for meals. With *Tell Me
Why*, I've got my own apartment, it's all furnished and
I'm staying up really late, and I'm drinking out of the
milk carton."

Wynonna Judd may be the most successful artist of
late to be just cutting the apron strings, but her second
album, *Tell Me Why*, has all the poise of a singer whose

"I heard a couple of songs I really loved and I could imagine myself bungee-jumping out into the audience."

"I heard a couple of songs I really liked and I could imagine myself bungee-jumping out into the audience."

name has become synonymous with the modern country sound.

"I go out and find songs that just hit me over the head and strike a chord in me," she explains. "If I hear a song that affects me, I do it. To me, there's two kinds of songs—good and bad."

Just as she took the natural approach in choosing songs, when Wynonna got into the studio, she trusted the songs to find their own best arrangements. "They just happen," she says, "and you just hope you can hang on. Some things happened very spontaneously on this album. The wonderful thing about (producer) Tony Brown is that he's real comfortable with spontaneity. We captured these moments as they happened. I believe in the live aspect of recording, and this is a very live album."

Several songs have direct connections to Wynonna's life. The slow, dark blues song, "That Was Yesterday," was written by Naomi. "I Just Drove By" evoked a familiar feeling in Wynonna, who frequently drives past the house where she and her mother used to live.

Though a lot was at risk when Wynonna began her solo career, any fears she had were offset by her excitement over beginning something new. "I feel like this is a fresh start," she says. "I can do whatever I want. The challenge is how far to push it without being dishonest. I heard a couple of songs I really loved and I could imagine myself bungee-jumping out into the audience. I had to stop and think, is this me? Do I want to wear this? Is this something that will fit me?"

—C.B. & K.F.

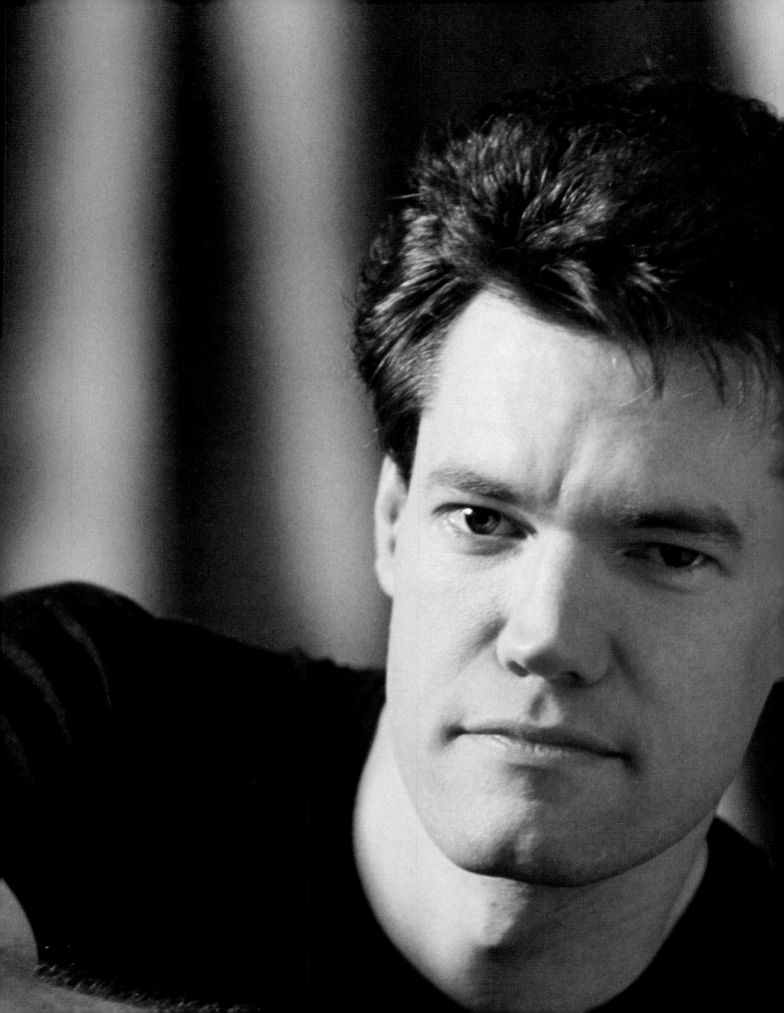

RANDY TRAVIS

HE PAVED THE WAY FOR COUNTRY'S NEW BREED

Randy Travis overcame a troubled youth to become one of today's most popular stars.

Photos courtesy of Warner Bros

Randy is the embodiment of country music—its sound, style, look, and attitude.

Twelve million albums, gold, platinum, every imaginable award—59, at the last count, hit singles, twelve Number 1's, an album at Number 1 for as long as 43 consecutive weeks. Randy Travis has accomplished more in six albums than most artists can dream of in a lifetime. Not bad for a guy who, in the beginning, couldn't have gotten a record deal if his life depended on it!

Randy Travis is the embodiment of country music—its sound, style, look, and attitude. On album as on stage, he delivers his goods with a cry, a wail, and a twang. He is credited with opening the door for "new traditionalist" artists like Alan Jackson, Garth Brooks, and Clint Black with the release of his 1986 debut, *Storms Of Life*. While this may very well be true, especially accurate is the fact that Randy Travis is also carrying on in the footsteps of his own idols: Hank Williams, Merle Haggard, George Jones.

Originally from North Carolina, he lived a rough and tumble lifestyle, and according to print stories, is described as a former juvenile delinquent who was looking at a five-year sentence for breaking and entering when manager Lib Hatcher was able to obtain custody of the teen. As the owner of a Charlotte club called

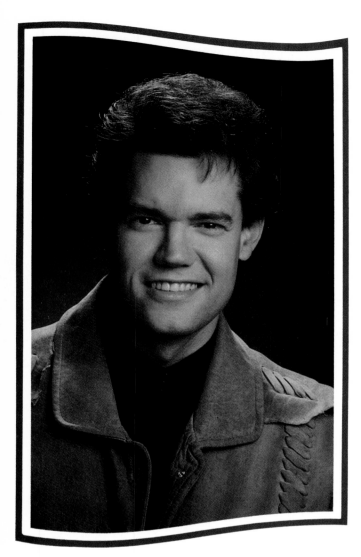

Since his success in the music industry, Randy has branched out into acting.

Travis's natural talents were shopped to every record label in town. They all turned him down.

Country City USA, she was convinced that the youngster had both talent and a future, and was determined not to let that combination slide off into lock-up.

Eventually, she sold the club, and relocated with the singer to Nashville, where he became a singing cook at the Nashville Palace, a well-known night spot near Opryland. Travis's natural talents were shopped to every record label in town, and in typical examples of record company brilliance and prescience of the next big thing, they all turned him down. Eventually, Warner Brothers caught on to the larger picture and inked him to a deal.

Repeatedly, Randy Travis was pointed out as being "too country" for the country music industry. (Record company logic again.) However, when *Storms Of Life* was released, it went platinum faster than any other debut by a country artist, proof positive that what the labels were delivering was not necessarily what the listening public had in mind. He quickly amassed every possible music award, including two Grammys and ten American Music Awards. His follow-up album, *Always And Forever,* stayed solid at Number One for ten months.

By 1990, he had made even more music history. He was named the Top Grossing Country Touring Artist Of The Year, and recorded an album of duets entitled *Heroes And Friends.* This gave him the chance to cut tracks with his personal heroes, such as George Jones, Tammy Wynette, B.B. King, Willie Nelson, and Roy Rogers. He continued touring, playing for sold-out crowds at every stop and gathering up more annual music awards.

His sixth album, *High Lonesome,* continues his long-standing reputation for quality songs and pensive delivery. But it also marks another milestone in Randy Travis's career. Five of the record's ten songs were co-written by the singer, who in the past had penned three hits: "I Told You So," "Reasons I Cheat," and the title track from *Heroes And Friends.* With *High Lonesome,* however, he has come into his own as a songwriting force, as well as forging a partnership with his touring-mate, Alan Jackson. Together, they collaborated on three of *High Lonesome*'s cuts: "Better Class Of Losers," "I'd Surrender All," and "Forever Together." Jackson also contributed "Allergic To The Blues."

In February, 1992, he started another leg of touring, as well as landing a part on the hit television series, *Matlock.* He flew to Hawaii to film portions of an upcoming television special, and continued his partnership with Feed The Children, in which a number of concert dates are attended by representatives of the charity to collect canned and non-perishable goods for distribution throughout that particular community.

With all the demands on his time, it's a wonder Randy Travis ever has a moment to himself. When he does, however, he spends it with manager/wife Lib Hatcher Travis at home, just twenty miles outside of Nashville. There, he de-stresses from industry pressures by weight-lifting or horseback riding, a passion he has enjoyed since his childhood in North Carolina.

Of country's many legends and superstars, Randy Travis has certainly earned his place at the top. He has paved the way for hopeful new talents, given his due to the stars that inspired him, and never disappointed fans with his creative output. He works diligently to maintain and surpass his levels of excellence, and delivers quality both on tape and on stage. His workaholic tendencies are paying off handsomely, both in terms of reviews and awards, and audience loyalty. If the late 1980's and early 1990's have given the music industry a true phenomenon, it is Randy Travis—a real credit to the values and traditions of his genre.—*E.H.*

Eighties new-traditionalism starts at Randy Travis' door!

BROOKS & DUNN

BOOGYIN'!

"There's nothing weird or complicated about the music we're trying to make," says Kix Brooks of Brooks & Dunn. "We're just cranking it up and going for a good time." While some groups have to concentrate on writing up-tempo numbers, Brooks & Dunn have to consciously try to slow down. "We get together and immediately start stirring it up," Brooks continues. "Before you know it, we're rockin'."

Playing a mixture of Southern rock and slightly left of mainstream country, the two have seen their audience grow steadily. "We love the arenas," Brooks admits. "But we won't forget where folks are in your face at the front of the stage. When we walk into those honky-tonks in the afternoon for our sound check, I always look around, take a deep breath, and say, 'Man, this is gonna be fun!' "

Fun seems to be in the boys' blood. Brooks grew up in Louisiana, where he lived down the block from country legend Johnny Horton. "That was my first exposure to gold records and things like that, so I got the bug way back," he says. Then Kix went to college to settle down, er, ah, I mean, to party it up. "It was when I got to college that I started seriously honky-tonkin', playing music all the time." He later took a year off and held jobs in various parts of the country, and did a lot of gigs. A longtime desire to play New Orleans led

Brooks & Dunn are one band whose working partnership has evolved into a good friendship.

48

Photo by Eddie Malluk

Photo by John Lee

to a stint there. He must have known what he was looking for. At one point, he played 72 nights in a row on Bourbon Street.

Brooks & Dunn have that rare kind of talent that only comes along once in a while. In a phrase, they work well together. All the songs on their album flow easily, and you know they're having as much if not more fun than their fans. They first tried writing together in Nashville. But their collaborations came out so well that their record label offered them a contract as performers.

"Musically, we feel things the same way," says Kix. "Ronnie leans a little closer to Lefty Frizzel and I might be a little more on the Glenn Frey side of things, but both of us like our country music with an edge to it. His voice might be a little more on the right and mine to the left, but they seem to have a nice meeting in the middle."

In a way, the Brooks & Dunn story sounds almost like a fairy tale. Brooks grew up country, and later wrote big hits for John Conlee, Nitty Gritty Dirt Band, and Highway 101. Dunn grew up pretty much the same way, falling easily into musical circles when he moved with his family to Tulsa, where he eventually led a band that headlined at one of the city's most popular nightspots.

Just two years ago, Brooks & Dunn roared onto the expanding country scene and lit a fire under everyone. Their debut album, *Brand New Man,* sold prodigiously and spawned four number one singles, "Brand New Man," "My Next Broken Heart," "Neon Moon," and the kicker, "Boot Scootin' Boogie," which became a crossover pop hit as well. Their high octane brand of pedal to the metal pickin' earned them a rabid following, and they seemed to have friends in both high and low places.

The world was watching when they released their follow-up album, *Hard Workin' Man.* "We tried to ignore whatever pressure there might have been," Dunn says. "We just did what worked the first time around—tried to come up with the best songs we could and record them as well as possible."

The result is that Brooks & Dunn have put an album that is quite similar on the surface, but this time, some of the best songs are ballads, while the up-tempo numbers remain raucous, loud and fun. "Hard Workin'

Brooks & Dunn say that they must consciously try to slow down, boogyin' is just what comes naturally.

Man" is a celebration of a guy with a superhuman work ethic, party ethic. It seems Brooks & Dunn might have burned a lot of rubber on *Brand New Man* and the subsequent double-time touring.

Shuffles and rockers like "We'll Burn That Bridge" and "Rock My World (Little Country Girl)" are infectious and fun, but the red hot pickin' doesn't really set in until "Texas Women (Don't Stay Lonely For Long)," midway through side two. Surprisingly, it's the ballads and mid-tempo songs that really shine on this album. "She Used To Be Mine" and "Mexican Minutes," with its tip of the hat to James Taylor, receive plenty of attention at the jukebox. But the heart-felt "That Ain't No Way To Go," about a woman who leaves without saying goodbye, and "Our Time Is Coming," a song of hope for the dispossessed and out of work, are truly memorable.

Whatever your pleasure, the songs on *Hard Workin' Man* provide plenty of exciting moments when Brooks & Dunn hit the road. The crowds are always waiting. "We're overwhelmed by the response," says Ronnie Dunn. "The crowds are like those at rock concerts—on their feet, raising Cain and having a great time from start to finish. There have been a couple of times that it's been so loud we couldn't hear the band over the crowd. It's just nuts!"

"We're outgrowing ourselves everywhere we look," Kix Brooks says with a combination of pleasure and concern, "from the band to crew to bus to truck—everything on every level. Our biggest challenge is just keeping up with ourselves. Not long ago, we were at a point where we could put a few boxes of t-shirts in the equipment truck. Now, our equipment truck is our t-shirt truck!"

"It's wonderful being able to make well-received records and videos," adds Dunn, "but there's nothing like walking out on that stage. The shows surpass records by far when it comes to excitement, fun and enjoyment." He pauses for a second and then shakes his head. "It's just a great thing to be a part of."

But their meteoric rise won't ever go unappreciated by the duo. "I've spent a lot of my of my life hauling around sound systems," Kix says with a laugh. "Ronnie and I really get to do our jobs now without having to worry about all that other stuff. It's very satisfying."—*C.B. & K.F.*

"It was when I got to college that I started seriously honky-tonkin'!"
— Kix Brooks

Photo by John Lee

Trisha's record *Hearts In Armor* featured guest appearances by Vince Gill, Emmylou Harris, Garth Brooks and Don Henley.

"They ask for autographs—it's strange to get that from people I grew up with."

TRISHA YEARWOOD

HOME TOWN GIRL DOES GOOD

Since the release of her self-titled debut album over two years ago, Monticello, Georgia native Trisha Yearwood experienced a No. 1 hit with her first single, "She's In Love With The Boy," two platinum records, and touring success. These things are beginning to sink in for the talented singer, who remarks, "Some days are better than others. It hits home when I'm not in a musical situation, when I'm not doing a concert, signing autographs. When those people are in line to see me, I'm used to it. They know Trisha Yearwood is there, and it feels normal. But when I'm at home in my sweats, with no makeup and my hair pulled up under a hat and someone walks up to me and says, 'Aren't you Trisha Yearwood?', that's when it hits me. The first time I got off a plane in Los Angeles and was recognized, I thought, 'Wow! People all over the country know who I am!'"

Home, she says, was a "small town of 2000 people. Everybody knows everybody, and five years ago, I couldn't walk down the street when I was home from college without having to stop for fifteen minutes at the grocery store to answer questions about my grades! Now, they ask me for autographs and take pictures, and it's strange to get that from the people I grew up with. It's a little different, but mostly they're proud that the home town girl did good. I don't get to spend much time there any more. I'm not in Georgia much, so my parents have to come to me. I live in Nashville and that's the only sacrifice I had to make. I was told up front that the first couple of years of my career, I would not be home. But if you work hard, it pays off, and then you can take some time for yourself. Maybe in another year, I can even take a vacation!"

She says she was very lucky to have supportive parents who encouraged her musical ambitions. "They trusted (my sister and me). We were good students

Despite her love for the music, Trisha Yearwood is the first to admit that "country music is a business."

with goals of getting educations. They didn't have to force us to go to college. If I had wanted to drop out, they would have been less than excited, but they knew I'd get a degree for myself and they encouraged both of us to do what made us happy and never think we had limitations. That was something they instilled in us, and when I told them what I wanted to do, they were behind me. My sister has a Master's in Animal Science, and I got my degree in Music Business. She just recently had her first baby, and that's ten times harder than what I do for a living! I would not trade for a second!"

When she moved to Nashville in 1985 to attend Belmont College, she was quickly exposed to the music industry. Yearwood interned at MTM Records for a year, and established a healthy career cutting demos and doing background vocals for the likes of Kathy Mattea and Garth Brooks. Still, it took six years from the time of her relocation until the signing of her own recording contract.

"A lot of it was me," she recalls. "I wasn't very aggressive; I didn't knock on doors. I've become aggressive about my career, but not about talking about myself, so it took longer than it could have. My main goal was to do this, but the first couple of years I was finishing college, then I got a job and didn't pound the pavement for a deal until Fall, 1988 or early 1989. It basically took two and a half years of real concentrated effort to make it happen. The rest of the time was spent waiting because I didn't know how to go about it. There are no books, they don't offer a course. You just have to jump in, and there is always that big fear of failing. I kept putting it off because I was afraid it might not happen. Finally, I decided it was time to just get off of my behind and jump in by doing demos to get my foot in the door. It worked.

"I did hundreds, maybe close to a thousand demos. They're all over the place. The main thing was, if I was recording a song that was going to be pitched to Reba McEntire or Wynonna Judd, I didn't try to sing it like they would. I didn't want to be pigeonholed. I sang it as if I were recording it for my own album. Even though there were a lot of different styles, everything I did, I put my own twist into and that helped me develop my own sound. It taught me what I wanted to do—record songs with a lot of power, emotion, and lyrics that I could sink my teeth into."

Out of those many sessions came songs that would eventually end up on her debut. "I did the original demo for 'Victim Of The Game' and wanted to record that before Garth Brooks did, but he had a deal first! 'When Goodbye Was A Word'—I demo'd that and it was real special to me because Gene and Paul Nelson wrote the song for themselves and had no idea who would ever record it. I took the rough copy out to the studio and played it for my producer, Garth Fundis. We try to cut things we are both excited about, and luckily, our tastes

are extremely similar. The rest of the songs got pitched to me along the way."

With the success of her first album under her belt, Trisha Yearwood came back with *Hearts In Armor*. Ten new songs of love and heartbreak from a country girl's perspective. Each song on *Hearts In Armor* contains its own style, from the country blues sound of "Wrong Side of Memphis" to the slow, soft ballad, "Nearest Distant Shore." Also included on Trisha's album are guest appearances by Garth Brooks, Vince Gill, Emmylou Harris, Raul Malo of the Mavericks, and Don Henley.

Through the rise of country music comes this new style and sound exemplified by Trisha Yearwood. With a strong singing voice, she tackles the problems that are inherent in a male dominated music scene.

Trisha's singing is not the only thing that stands out on her albums. Her lyrics also deliver a cutting edge, especially with songs like "Walkaway Joe," which is the story of a young woman's unfortunate infatuation with a reckless, worthless man. "My lyrics are geared to the independent woman," she says, "I made a record that was me."

That is exactly how Yearwood presents it on *Hearts In Armor*. Trisha proves herself to be a contemporary woman who takes no slack and avoids falling into sexist stereotypes. "There have been certain subjects in the past that women haven't been able to speak about. But I have not had to compromise what I sing about at all."

Another track that stands out on this record is, "You Don't Have to Move that Mountain" featuring Vince Gill. It's an enlightening, spiritual song that's refreshing and new. It's not often that we hear such songs in today's modern music.

Trisha's unique style of country is a result of her growing up on Elvis, Linda Ronstadt, and the Eagles, as opposed to Merle Haggard and George Jones. "Anything I sing sounds country, but I wanted it to have a little bit of that edge from back then, so that's what we went for," she says, speaking of her early influences.

Trisha Yearwood is not just a pretty woman with a beautiful voice. She is very involved in her career and her own business. She has a degree in business administration and she states that, "Country music is a business. I'm the head of a corporation and my name is the bottom line. Even now I spend one and a half to two hours a day singing and the rest of the time is business. Gone are the days of artists totally neglecting the business side and getting taken for a ride."

With Trisha Yearwood, you have a "country girl," who is also a modern day independent woman with a good head on her shoulders, and an excellent singer. She stands out as one of the most promising female vocalists in country music today. With both her albums gone platinum, Trisha is guaranteed to be at the top of country music for years to come.—*E.H. & J.P.*

Trisha with guitarist Johnny Garcia.

Before hitting the big time Trisha Yearwood sang songwriters' demos for the likes of Garth Brooks, Reba McEntire and the Judds.

AARON TIPPIN
WORKING MAN'S HERO!

Many of his songs have become anthems for blue collar groups.

Over the course of two albums, Aaron Tippin quickly established himself as the working man's hero. Many of his songs, most notably "You've Got To Stand For Something" and "I Wouldn't Have It Any Other Way" have become anthems for both blue collar groups and defenders of individuality. Tippin's latest release, *Call Of The Wild,* jumped right into his continuing theme with tracks like "Working Man's Ph.D" and "Trim Yourself To Fit The World."

Three albums—how do you see each as a step in your natural growth?

The most evident thing goes without saying, and you get that from nothing more than experience. When I got the deal, my first album was nothing more than "Hey, I think this is great country music! What do you folks think?" It did decent; it's almost gold. I came at the second album from watching the audience and listening to them in audience lines. Things always change. I had more influence on producing the third album, so you hear more of my type of music, not just lyrically. I still listen to what country fans want to hear. I'm always building and narrowing the process. Every album is more and more Aaron Tippin music.

You were a songwriter in Nashville for five years before getting a deal. How valuable was that experience in preparing you for this?

Very valuable. I was a lucky guy who spent just the right amount of time as a songwriter. I studied the craft long enough to know what makes a great country song, but not long enough to be unable to go up the highway at 60 miles per hour. I'm glad I was a songwriter first because it is almost impossible to do it the other way around. There is too much to do in front of your career: My computer is on, reporting radio stations are in my card file, I call and thank them for playing my new

single, do interviews, deal with my road crew, my company, then I have a writing appointment this afternoon. I'm very grateful I spent time learning to be a songwriter. It taught me how to keep on being one.

What makes a great country song?

I don't want anyone to think I'm some smart-aleck who knows what it takes! I think I write good songs and by the same token, anyone who's been doing this, even for 50 years, will tell you—you write bad ones too! It's a matter of culling out, making the message clear. Here is Aaron Tippin's philosophy: Two things are mighty important. (1) Say something country fans want to hear, that makes them turn up the radio and relate. (2) I can relate to the song, take part of my life and apply it. I say exactly what I think. Those are the two principals that always apply when I write a song,

Aaron drives a Chevy Turbo pick-up truck, which he considers to be one of the perks of his job.

Call Of The Wild is not only the name of Tippin's latest record, it's also the title of a collection of his videos.

On songwriting, Aaron Tippin's philosophy is
1) say something country fans want to hear and
2) make sure it's something you can relate to.

whether it's good or bad. Not by any means do I think I'm the greatest songwriter. I am immediately humbled in the presence of Max D. Barnes and Whitey Shafer, and I know my place in the pecking order! In this stage, a super song passes by like sunlight and I try to snatch it when it's there. Max and Whitey— the sun shines on them all the time!

I was speaking with a heavy metal publicist in Los Angeles and your name came up. She told me how much her brother loves you, that he and his friends were going to see you in concert there. Could this have happened ten years ago?

That is it—we are having a boom and I think it's because first of all, we're hearing some of the greatest country songs in history on the radio and it gives the rest of us a great opportunity. New ears came to country through "Achy Breaky Heart"—ten million records! Garth Brooks brought a lot of people. The old stereotype that country music is about crying in your beer is over. I always said give me every sad song in country and I'll find you one on the pop charts. I called it the 1970's attitude to country. It has changed, and that's wonderful. The younger generation is a lot smarter than my generation. I was prejudiced the other way—I wouldn't listen to anything but country and my friends all listened to rock and roll. Now the days of peer pressure are not the case. You can be in the drive-through at Burger King and have one car playing rap and a pickup playing George Strait right behind it. They like what they like in spite of their friends and appreciate a lot more music than we do. I got in a pickup truck to hear a guy's sound system. He picked up my CD and right next to it he had MC Hammer. This generation can show us all something!

Photo by Frank Okenfels

Photo by Frank Okenfels

What is it like growing up in Traveler's Rest, South Carolina?

Traveler's Rest is actually the closest town to where I'm from. I grew up in the hills three miles to the state line where my mom lives. It's hillbilly country. People there are quiet to strangers, very family-oriented. If you have a hillbilly for a neighbor and he likes you, he'll do anything for you. But if he doesn't you need to move off somewhere else! I think the hardest decision I ever made in my life was to leave home. I can still see the hill I sat on, trying to decide whether to do it or not. I never had a one-horse town attitude. I still think it's the greatest place on earth. It tore me apart to leave the family and friends I grew up with.

Is that where your work ethic was instilled?

It was. I was raised on a farm and by age seven, my dad turned me loose with the tractor on a 90-acre hay field and expected me to have it done. I was taught responsibility at a very young age, and taught to fly planes, so I've always looked for and tried to live up to responsibility.

When success happens, is it hard to retain your roots or convince the folks back home that you haven't lost your down to earth simplicity?

I hope I haven't. The other night, I was eating at a Waffle House in Hilton Head; the night before last, at a local Nashville restaurant. I think it's important to keep a firm foot in where you came from. I got to where I am not by what I'm going to be, but by what I was. That keeps me in touch. In some cases you read stories about yourself that sound so great you've got to be careful not to believe it! If there's anything special about Aaron Tippin, it's my God-given talent. I decided I would work hard to use it. Past that, I'm no different.

My pickup truck is a little nicer: a Chevy turbo diesel. But if you move off so far to the secluded world of being a star, you forget who you're doing this for and your career takes a turn for the worse. It's a funny thing about the public—they fire you and don't tell you. They just walk off and leave you standing there to find out on your own.

You sign autographs every night after the show. What is the longest you've spent, and why is it important for you to meet everyone in the audience rather than hold a selective meet and greet like other artists do?

My Fan Fair party this year, I signed for seven and a half hours. On the road, it's anywhere from an hour to three and a half. It varies with conditions. The other night, we spent an hour in the pouring rain. First of all, I believe that fans are the most important people. They are my customers. I enjoy and want to spend as much time with them as I can. One on one is the most important marketing tool ever found. They are super-honest people who tell you what they like and don't like. If I want to know what to put on my next album, I just add and subtract!—*E.H.*

MARK CHESNUTT

COUNTRY'S RISING STAR

"The studio just gets me nervous."

Playing over 200 dates a year, Mark Chesnutt is a busy man. His three albums, *Too Cold At Home, Longnecks And Short Stories* and *Almost Goodbye,* have earned him a string of hit singles, including several No. 1's. Likewise, he has been featured in virtually every magazine and newspaper across the country. In 1992, he beat Gerardo, Vanilla Ice and Chris Isaak for the AMOA award of Rising Star, given for jukebox play and 1993 saw him win the coveted CMA Horizon Award. Talented, quick-witted, and sharp, Mark Chesnutt is pushing aside the competition without even trying. So impressive, in fact, is this young Texan that his hero, George Jones, even wrote the liner notes for his debut.

While airplay and jukeboxes have been more than generous to his recorded sound, Chesnutt says the studio is one place he still can't call home. "It's like night and day from there to the stage," he observes. "I don't feel I do my best work in the studio. I don't know why; I guess it's because I've spent so many years performing. The studio just gets me nervous. It's the one place where if you screw up, you can do it over, but it feels unnatural. I think I'm getting better at it though."

Chesnutt began playing clubs when he was sixteen, receiving tremendous support and encouragement from his father, also a singer/recording artist. The late Bob Chesnutt gave his son the confidence to make repeated trips to Nashville, seek out quality songs, and cut demos. One of these trips proved fateful in the upcoming star's future, when he landed upon the title track to

Mark Chesnutt is the winner of the
1993 CMA Horizon award.

61

Country legend George Jones was so impressed by Chesnutt that he wrote the liner notes for Chesnutt's debut album.

Too Cold At Home. He explains, "(Songwriter) Bobby Harden played a big part in my getting a record deal because he held that song for me. On my second album, 'Old Country' and 'Talking To Hank' (which features George Jones) were songs he also held for me for several years. It has gotten to where I can tell a Bobby Harden song when I hear one. He says simple things with simple words; his writing is totally different from anyone else's."

When it comes to selecting just the right tunes, Chesnutt says the primary criteria is, "It has to hit me the first time I hear it. Two or three lines into it, I know if it's for me. It has to have the right words, the melody has got to stick with me. If I find myself humming it all day, chances are everyone else will do the same."

He agrees that country music has, of late, become a crowded field, but is confident that the industry is not about to suffer another "Urban Cowboy" craze, with every Ph.D. driving around in a BMW, sporting a western hat and boots, and riding the mechanical bull Friday nights at the local disco-turned-country club.

"This is more valid," he asserts. "Last time, it wasn't real. It was all because of a movie, and the songs back then weren't even really country. It was a fad. This has been coming on for a long time. I've seen it for a few years with all the new artists coming in. People like Clint Black, Garth Brooks—especially Garth, helped a lot; he brought in new people to the shows. Also, the record companies are branching out more and not trying to stay within the bounds of country music. They are trying to appeal to everyone.

"A lot of young people, I think, got tired of heavy metal, rap, and other kinds of music. They started listening to country and have decided it's just better. I don't see it stopping. Everything comes and goes, but country music has always been here, and I think more people are going to start listening to it because it's fun now and not corny. It's upbeat and there is a lot of great talent out there. It used to be that country shows were kind of boring, but the young entertainers are putting more energy into it. Before, it was just not acceptable to shake your butt on stage, and now it's looked upon as just having a good time. Country music has caught on—when you go to the shows, there are so many young people screaming, getting excited—you can't hold back; you've got to really cut loose! Years ago, a lot of older people went to the shows and they weren't that rowdy. Now, they like anything you do!"

With competition increasing on a daily basis as more and more fresh faces are signed and thrown into the sea of albums, Chesnutt says it's no secret what an artist needs to stand out. "One thing: great music. You've got to have the songs, the right management, someone who knows how to market and put you above everyone else. You've got to have a great video and album, but you need radio airplay because if they don't touch you, you're nobody. You can't not worry. You've got to work for that airplay, and really call and visit all those stations. I worry a lot; I don't just say, 'Here it is; here's my record.' Luckily, I've been around a while and met every country radio station. I have a good relationship with them and so far, they've played everything I've put out."

Photo by M. Rutherford/courtesy of MCA records

"If people look at me as another hat act, that's fine. I've been called worse."

Success, he admits, has resulted in a few lifestyle changes. "I'm a lot busier now," he observes. "I'm hardly ever home. But I'm the same guy I was a few years ago. I know that because I still get along with all my friends and they tell me. The schedule I have to keep is sometimes ridiculous. I think I'm making money; I know I'm spending a hell of a lot! I'm able to do things I've always wanted to do. TNN's 'Celebrity Outdoors' paid for me to go fishing in Florida; I'm going to Alaska to fish for pleasure, I bought my mother her first new car, I've bought land to build a house on—a house I'll be in eventually, when I get to the point where I can work 100 dates a year! But I get bored easily, so I like the road a lot. I enjoy being out working."

Asked if he is comfortable with the term "celebrity," he muses, "I don't think about it much, really. I guess if people say I am, fine. It's better than being thought of as a nobody." As far as his image is concerned, if he has one and if so, what it is, he candidly remarks, "I don't know, to tell the truth. I don't know how people see me, whether it's a good old boy or a rowdy redneck or a nice quiet guy. I need to ask somebody! I'd like to think it's as a good country singer and entertainer. I never thought about it because if I tried to project an image, then I would have to try to live up to it all the time. Now, I'm just me doing what I love and trying to do my best. If people look at me as 'another hat act,' that's fine—I've been called worse!"—*E.H.*

George Jones, Merle Haggard and Hank Williams are Joe's primary musical influences.

JOE DIFFIE
HONKY-TONK WITH ATTITUDE

"I wrote about good stuff happening when you go to a honky tonk and the fun you can have."

Joe Diffie had no idea he was coining a new phrase in the English language when he wrote the title track to his album, *Honky Tonk Attitude,* but three albums and a lot of years into his career, nothing comes as a surprise. After all, this is a man who once remarked, "My whole life is an accident." Out on the road—where he spends most of his time—Diffie phoned to offer insight on basically any subject that came to mind!

What is a "Honky Tonk Attitude?"

Oh, I knew you were going to ask that. Everyone asks that and there's no good answer. I just wrote a song with that line in it. It revolved around fun, being yourself, belly rubbing, drinking, dancing, whooping and hollering. That's what I envision. I wrote about good stuff happening when you go to a honky tonk and the fun you can have.

Do real honky tonks still exist?

I don't know. I guess they still exist; they do in small towns. Go to Stella's in Velma, Oklahoma—if you don't have a gun, they give you one on your way in! I remember one time I was practicing at my friend's house, my pick-up broke down, we walked to Stella's and she wouldn't let us in, even though she knew who we were. She said, "Get away! I've got a shotgun!" "We're broke down. Can you call this number for us?" "No!" She was rather rude about it. But I think the stereotype is changing. People now perceive honky tonks as western dance clubs. At least I think so. I don't know—I'm not a honky tonkologist!

Do you dance in these places?

No. I made the mistake once. I was with a music business friend at a club somewhere after a show and she said, "My daughter would get a kick out of dancing with you." So I did it and 30 women came up and wanted to dance with me. I said, "I can't" and got the cussing out of my life: "You think you're too good!" "You sorry S.O.B.!" I got out of there and resolved never again unless I'm with my wife.

What's your step of choice? Line dance? Two-step?

I provide the music for line dancing. I do a very basic two-step, just barely enough to call it that. I had to dance on the dadgummed *Vicki!* show on national television, plus she kept going on and on about that "hunk" thing—it was embarrassing.

Although his own music is used constantly for line dances, Joe says his own dancing prowess is limited to a very basic two-step.

Photo courtesy of Sony Music

With the release of his latest record, Joe added a new term to the English language.

Were you really turned down by a record executive who said he would have signed you if you looked like George Strait?

I was signed by that same guy. He said if I looked like Strait he would have signed me sooner. I can accept that. I don't like it, but I accept it. He was an A&R guy and my producer and I appreciated his honesty. He said, "No one sings like you, but you need to lose weight." I did and he signed me. Unfortunately, looks play a huge role in this visual medium. See who's hot and it's based by and large on how they look, regardless of how they sing. The majority of record buyers are females 12 to 18. That's why females have a harder time in this business and hunks have a little easier time. It's a game you've got to play along with.

Keeping in mind, of course, that if these same guys bagged groceries for a living, women wouldn't give them the time of day. (No offense to grocery baggers!)

I never understood. It's like that Alabama song trying to figure out what girls like about boys in the band. There's just something about that. Not saying women are superficial, of course!

Neither are men—it's not like all women are expected to look like centerfolds.

Hal Ketchum said something in an interview that I appreciate and have taken to heart. He said when he started out, the label tried pushing him as a sex symbol and he said, "I'm tired of trying. I'm just me." People see the artificiality of the event and what you strive for is just to look as good as you can and do music the best you can, and if a woman thinks you're sexy and gorgeous, that's wonderful too.

Are you still working out two hours a day?

No more. I play a lot of golf, basketball, work out occasionally. I did two hours every day to get down to a certain weight and it's hard to find time, so I do other activities, try to eat right. My weight fluctuates up and down ten pounds. I change every day and that's what I like about this business—there is no regimentation. I get up when I want, do what I've got to do, interviews, television, play basketball. I like that freedom. I'm not as heavy into diet. I eat low-fat, and occasionally I have pizza, but I watch it. I cannot live on baked chicken and rice; I refuse. I eat what I want, but not as much of it. It works pretty well. With regular exercise and being careful, I can maintain.

Exercise, healthy diet . . . and a pack a day smoker? Something's not right!

Along with the freedom comes a lot of spare time and with eight or nine hours on a bus, there's only so many movies you can watch—so you smoke. I don't recommend it to anyone and I wish I could quit, but I haven't mastered it. I tried the patches, but I couldn't keep them lit!

Where would you like to be a year from now?

Good question. Hopefully doing the same thing, more of the same, and more successful than before. I don't know how that would feel—I've done well, achieved a lot, but you're never satisfied. Musicians are all co-dependents; we're people pleasers who want more. We all want to be adored and that's why we do what we do. It's humbling to go to award shows; fans are in the audience, they holler for you, then someone else gets an ovation and it's "Oh my God—I know where I stand!" Did you hear about the co-dependent country musician? When he died, he wanted Garth Brooks' life to flash before his eyes!

No doubt!!!

But I can't be jealous of someone that successful because he has helped others as much as himself. He has brought more awareness to country music and on top of that, he's a hell of a nice guy, a real good guy, so you can't resent someone like that.

What kind of feedback do you get from your fans?

They're real free with their opinions. The other night, this woman came back—she'd been to 40 shows—and she whispered, "Your band looked horrible tonight! They weren't well dressed at all!" I said, "Okay." What can you say to that? Some people say, "Cut your hair," some say, "Your hair is long and beautiful." There are two sides to every issue. There is always someone with another side and they'll tell you about it, on any subject. One lady didn't like the light show. The light was in her eyes and she couldn't see. She wrote to me, the record label, Ralph Emery—"Tell Joe." You do this to add to your show so people will hopefully like it better, and she didn't! Then you see the nicest letters, glowing letters to magazines: "Joe Diffie is the nicest human being on Earth." One lady wrote to my fan club—of which she was not a member: I played a show, signed autographs for two hours afterward backstage with a 700-mile drive ahead of me and we were already late. She wrote that she traveled 200 miles and she didn't get an autograph and how could I treat my fans that way? You can't please everyone—I've come to that conclusion.

So what is the solution?

Please yourself. It's all you can do. Ultimately it comes down to doing what makes you happy. You're not responsible for everyone else's happiness.

What makes you happy?

Knowing I've done a good show, sang well, collected the money—several times I didn't!—people are pleased, people I worked with are pleased. We get so many compliments because we have such a great crew: "Best sound, best show we've ever seen." It's a nice feeling to know that.

Even though he is considered a country-hunk, Diffie was originally told that he'd have to change his appearance in order to get signed.

What's the best piece of advice you were ever given?

My dad told me, and this applies to music or anything: "If you have a goal, you've got to do something every day toward that goal." It's easier to say than do, but he told me to go to Nashville, play, sing, meet people. That's what I did and it worked for me. Of course, you've got to realize that if you want to be a country singer and you can't carry a tune . . . if you look like George Strait you might have a shot! But fans are too smart and eventually it will come out. The letters and comments I get—people perceive me as real and down to earth, and I thank God I can sing a little!—*E.H.*

MARTY STUART
MASTER OF THE CRAFT

Born in Philadelphia, Mississippi, Marty Stuart was four years old when he received his first guitar. At age nine, he was playing Johnny Cash songs note for note; a few years later, he began his professional career on tour with Lester Flatt.

"It wouldn't have happened with The Rolling Stones," he states of leaving home at 13. "It took a guy like Lester Flatt, who gave me a home, allowed me to keep 30 dollars a week and send the rest to my mother to put in the bank, and made sure my schoolwork was completed by correspondence. It was a very business-like deal, not 'Hey Mom, I'm leaving.' My mother was an ambitious person who felt confined in Philadelphia, Mississippi. She knew I had that same ambition, that I wanted to shake hands with the world, and I love her for that."

Stuart's debut, *Busy Bee Cafe,* was released in 1982 on Sugar Hill Records. In 1986, he was signed to CBS Records, where a self-titled album failed to make waves. Its follow-up, *Let There Be Country,* failed to

Aside from his own hit singles, Marty Stuart has also penned songs for
many of today's top country artists.

Photo courtesy of MCA Records

Singer/guitarist/songwriter/reporter/
photographer/music historian—
ladies and gentlemen, Marty Stuart!

"I don't care where a hit comes from as long as it's a hit. I was forced into writing my own. I wasn't selling back then, and I couldn't expect great songwriters to give me their best so they could go to Number 50 and die. I knew I was a different kind of entertainer with a different point of view, and the songs would have to come from me and a writer or two who could see what I do. I thought 'Hillbilly Rock' and 'Cry Cry Cry' would be bigger than they were. I completely missed the mark on those, and as a result, decided the best thing is to record ten songs I love and let the label release what it will."

One of country music's most vibrant live performers, Stuart is surprisingly low key when he's not behind a microphone. "I save my energy all day for that hour onstage," he once explained. "It's like coming home to a revival. Music lights me up."

Despite winning music awards and being championed across the pages of national publications, he maintains a down to earth grip, never forgetting his roots. He applies this philosophy to every aspect of his life.

He observes, "I take the viewpoint that musicians are all wired backwards and there are enough of us in this alternative society to make it fashionable. Every human being on earth has something to offer. It doesn't matter if I'm sitting in front of a country store whittling, or in New York City talking to a guy who runs drugs for Libya. Music is my trade, everybody has one, and I have no problems with that. We all live on the same Earth and I don't feel that anyone is more special. It goes back to people's hearts. If they have good motives, I have no problem getting along with them. I don't like posers or jerks; I have no time for them. I like real people."

As far as stardom is concerned, he draws his own conclusion, noting that it is "nothing more than hard work. It's a hard job and a lot of sacrifices. What keeps me together is getting in my jeep with my bloodhound, driving off, and talking to God. I fish; I go to Wal-Mart. This is 33 years of love for country music, a combination of my influences and my talent. I just call myself a state-of-the-art struggling hillbilly singer."

Those years have earned Marty Stuart the respect of the music industry, and taught him great discipline in his craft. "I take most of January to do nothing but write," he explains. "I become like a street guy and writer. I get away. You shouldn't beat writing out like a nine-to-five job. There are guys who do that every day in Nashville. But my favorite way is walking down the road and feeling it, then taking it to paper. I like to be myself and get truly inspired by good or hard times."

surface until the label saw fit to cash in on his current success. By the time he signed with MCA—the beginning of a string of hits—he had recorded a collaborative gospel disc with Jerry and Tammy Sullivan, *A Joyful Noise,* became a reporter/photographer for *Country Music Magazine,* and gained respect as an encyclopedia of country music history and one of its strongest supporters.

By the time he released *This One's Gonna Hurt You* in 1992, Stuart was spinning heads as a musician, performer and songwriter—a skill he enjoys sharing, and once described as, "Almost like thinking, 'I've got to write my mother a letter. Who can write it with me?' You need someone with the same musical vision, someone you enjoy playing music with, and someone who has a tape recorder better than yours! That's hard to find. It's like looking for friends—you wind up with one or two, and a whole room of acquaintances.

"First of all, I think songs truly are a gift from God. They are heaven-sent or a hell-sent piece of business, and God is the best writer we ever had. He tends to put people together. I depend on my radar to tell me . . . It's like meeting a girl: You know instantly if you like her or don't. How to find a co-writer—It's an impossible question to answer.

MARY-CHAPIN CARPENTER
NEVER HAD IT SO GOOD!

Mary-Chapin Carpenter's fourth album, *Come On, Come On* was as consistent an award winner as her previous albums, but its success does not rely on hit formulas. Mary-Chapin has an uncanny ability to probe the darker side of human nature, and this talent endears her to fans.

Her easy-going, self-effacing manner belies a somber soul. "There's a melancholy, and sometimes it grabs you and won't let go, and other times it's lightened itself and you can go on, but it's like a trail that you leave behind you," she reveals.

Does she feel as miserable as her songs sometimes suggest? "Well, yes, I do tend to dwell on the dark side of things. I write about things I know about: depression, guilt, despair, failed relationships, you know. But everybody has moments of despair; it's just that I exploit mine."

Writing gut-wrenching lyrics is therapy for Carpenter, like a musical diary. "Believe me, I haven't been a total failure in matters of the heart. But you know how it is: The less pleasant, more drama-oriented scenarios have more of an edge to them, don't they? And writing for me is a cathartic process, so when I'm feeling bad, I write about it. When I'm enjoying myself, I don't have time."

At age 26, Mary-Chapin battled alcohol addiction. "I had a big problem. It was awful. I had to make a lifestyle change in a drastic way. It's still so painful to me to think about how I was." Coinciding with her alcohol problems was a severe musical slump. "I was more and more aware of the fact that I was keeping my singing job to buy beer. I mean, I was sitting there doing other people's music because it made me happy, and now I was miserable, just utterly empty. That was a time of great sadness, insecurity, questioning and crisis."

What resulted from the turmoil Carpenter experienced contributed to her artistic success. Finding an ally in guitarist John Jennings gave her the necessary boost to launch her career. After making demos of her

Mary-Chapin Carpenter originally hails from the un-country town of Princeton, New Jersey.

Photo courtesy of Sony Music

Carpenter's musical weight comes from years of inner struggle and growth.

"The truth is that the first song that got on the radio I drew from this one relationship is a song called 'Never Had It so Good.' I never imagined that it would get on the radio. I never meant to embarrass anybody. Songwriting is a personal endeavor, self-therapy, if you will."

Carpenter's mentor John Jennings grounds her. "He's my toughest and most honest critic. Over time we have developed this intuitive artistic relationship. I trust him to be utterly straightforward about whether something works. It puts hair on your chest, that kind of back and forth. It keeps you sharp, saves you from complacency."

According to Carpenter, "The songs come quickly. I don't write on the road. I have no set agenda. I present 10 or 12 songs that reflect what I'm thinking. The themes don't emerge until you have a whole." Carpenter is reluctant to get more specific about the songwriting process. There are many artists and producers she'd like to work with, but refuses to name them as "it all depends on the nature of the project." As to what kinds of projects: "I'd like to make an all-acoustic album and do the collaborative thing with other writers—all projects that feed the art monster." Other than that, she remains vague about her future plans.

Carpenter's commitment shows through in her political involvement. She worked on 'Til Their Eyes Shine: The Lullaby Album with Gloria Estefan, Carole King, Dionne Warwick, Emmylou Harris, and Roseanne Cash. The proceeds benefit the Institute for Cultural Understanding, an organization that works with children and teaches that tolerance is the first step toward avoiding violence.

Carpenter believes that being political isn't a conscious step you take at certain age; it's inherent in human nature. "What's wrong is lack of political awareness and young people feeling voter apathy. Asking 'Are you political?' is like 'do you use deodorant?' or 'are you a woman?'"

One artist Carpenter admires is k.d. lang. "She's responsible for persuading people that it's not just someone's look, image, or material. She's one of the great singers, interpreters of music. She's pushed the edge of the envelope. By following her artistic muse, she's been shut out by the establishment. Steve Earl, Lyle Lovett, and Nanci Griffith have all had similar trouble. The format hasn't fully accepted those other artists, and it's country music's loss."

Carpenter feels "lucky to have gotten support and airplay from country radio. I feel fortunate to have gotten a deal out of Nashville when it was opening up to singers-songwriters." And with Mary-Chapin Carpenter's genre-bending music, she's continuing the current glasnost with the Nashville establishment.—K.F.

songs in Jennings' D.C. basement, she wasted no time landing a deal with CBS Records with unprecedented control over the production of her albums. With Jennings' help, she went against conventional country wisdom and cut the album far from Nashville supervision.

"I have absolutely nothing against Nashville production. I feel quite strongly, though—and I feel a sense of pride about this—that you don't have to be in Nashville to make a good country record, or for that matter be in New York to make a good rock record or L.A. to make a good pop record. I just disagree with the idea that you have to work in a particular place to make a viable-sounding piece of work in a genre that's become identified with that place. If the music is written with a certain feeling in a certain style and executed as such, it shouldn't matter where you do it."

Nor does she feel confined to one musical idiom. She expresses what she feels in the rhythms best suited for each emotion, and her music can range from acoustic country to folk to pop-rock. Sometimes in delving into her past, she forgets that her private life is on display.

DOUG STONE
ALWAYS A COUNTRY SINGER

Ask country sensation Doug Stone to cite his primary musical influence and he's likely to say, "Mom." A singer and guitarist in her own right, his mother took him along to her many gigs and had him on stage when he was a mere seven years old. "She taught me to play guitar and sing," the Georgia native recalls. "She had a loud voice and like her, I really push; I give one hundred percent. She saw that I was intrigued by music when I was three or four years old, and she offered to teach me guitar and voice. I taught myself keyboards, bass, and drums and just kept going from there." By the age of sixteen, he had built the first of six home recording studios, where he would cut demos, "for insight on what I sounded like, my way, not trying to sound like anyone else."

He has vivid recollections of his first moment in front of an audience. "It was at East Point Auditorium, in Georgia. Then, when I was between the ages of seven and eleven, I was playing drums, and my mother was singing with the Country Rhythm Playboys. They would tape a radio show every Sunday, and she brought me along. The next oldest guy in the band was 34, but I got a job with them! I started recording with them in their little studio, an eight-track, for W Records and Bobby Whitley in Lawrenceville. He had a studio and a music store, a really nice guy."

When Stone's parents divorced, he moved with his mother to Newnan, Georgia (ironically, also the home of Alan Jackson, although the two would not meet until years later, when they were both in Nashville). "My friend and I started a band," he explains. "Chet and I played together forever, and he bought a four-track studio. I bought one as well and we combined them to put our resources together. We were mostly playing rock and roll and pop music, although I would occasionally do a country song, which flipped my mother out; she'd say, 'Now you're getting it!'

Doug Stone taught himself to play piano, bass and drums and built his own home recording studio by the age of sixteen.

"Of course, the 1970's pop music has turned into the country music of the 1990's. People in the industry don't like to hear that, but it's true. A band like The Eagles today would be considered a country group. I never considered, even back then, a rock and roll life. I like rock and roll; I like all music, but I was always a country singer. I auditioned once for a pop band; it was more rock and roll than pop, and they said, 'You've got a good voice, but you're definitely a country singer.' It didn't hurt my feelings, because really, I knew.

"I also played in a dance band, playing disco, funk, rock, pop and soul. That was with Chet and a guy named Steve. I don't know where either of them are now. We got older, married, divorced, or had kids—whatever. Life takes its course, you move away, and you lose touch. Being on the road, there is no time to keep up. You hock everything, drop it all to do this—or else you don't do it. It takes a lot of dedication."

During this period, he also became seasoned behind the boards, a talent he considers invaluable. "It was trial and error, reading the manuals. There was no one to tell me anything. The first time I bought a compressor, I overdid it. It was a matter of training my ears, a hands-on deal, listening while turning the knobs for the actuality of what they do. You have to do more than read the book or go to school and have someone tell you. I loved what I was doing and I stayed with it. Now it helps me in the studio because it gives me my sound over anyone else. The music is that distinct."

The road to success came through determination, and for Stone, by staying close to home. "It's fate; that's the only thing I can say," he modestly explains. "In this business, I found out, it's eighty percent luck and twenty percent talent, with a lot of hard work. I was playing a VFW club in Newnan when a woman named Phyllis Bennett came to see me from North Carolina on the advice of some friends. She loved the way I sang and became my manager." Within two years, Stone had a record deal.

"My producer played three songs we did for Epic and he brought me up there to play with my guitar. That was the beginning. I felt positive from that moment, and have been lucky that people like my music. I really did it all from home, a different route. I built my studio and have a backlog of tapes that you wouldn't believe! They are special to me because they mark the shaping and molding of my career with no one telling me, 'That's wrong.' Stanley Jordan—nobody told him what to do. He did it his way and is extraordinary. If you go after it by yourself, you will go further than with someone telling you, 'You can't do that!' My attitude was always, 'I can if I want to!' My dad showed me what life is about, and gave me the drive to do what I wanted: set a goal and strive for it. Of course, he told me I'd never make it in the music business, but I got the chance to show

Photo courtesy of Sony Music

him, which has been neat!"

True to form, Stone is one of the few holdouts on relocating to Music City. "I'm not moving to Nashville," he states, "just to Tennessee at the Kentucky border. From my property, I can see Kentucky. My wife loves horses, and I've been trying to get back to the country since I was five."

As for his career, being versatile on vocals, production, and a multitude of instruments gives him special insight when it comes to making records. "I direct!" he laughs. "That is my part now. I can't play as well as those (musicians); it's hard to beat a man at his own game. I listen, they know what they're doing. and if I hear a lick, I say so and they play it. More or less, I hum real good! I let the band play in the studio and they say I hum great!

"Basically, I just do what I do and hope the people like it, because it's all I can do. A leopard can't change his spots. I'm just thankful to God for my fans, otherwise, if not for them, I would still be twisting wrenches under a truck. There are a million people out there who can do what I do, and do it better. I just got a shot and I've run with it consistently. I'm not quitting until they say I'm through!"—E.H.

ALABAMA
AT HOME
AT NUMBER 1!

They are unquestionably the biggest group in country music, and one of the biggest in music history. Alabama: Randy Owen, Teddy Gentry, Jeff Cook and Mark Herndon are superstars, and they have the statistics to prove it. Album sales of over 45 million, over 30 Number One singles, 150 music awards including two Grammys, eight Entertainer of the Year awards, and Artist of the Decade. And it took them barely over ten years to do it. Of those 30 hits, 21 were consecutive from 1980 through 1987, an unbroken record that will probably never be equaled. Thanks to Alabama, country music opened its doors to bands instead of simply solo artists, and the genre found a home among fans of all tastes and demographics.

First cousins Owen and Gentry, with distant cousin Cook, began playing together as Young Country, and Wild Country three years later. Maintaining day jobs and pursuing degrees, they became full-time musicians in 1973, hired as houseband at The Bowery in Myrtle Beach, the city that today houses Alabama's own music theatre.

During the Bowery days, they went through a string of drummers until auditioning Massachusetts native Herndon, a former rock and roll player who joined the band in 1979, two years after an independent record deal gone under. In 1980, Alabama was signed to RCA on the heels of a rousing performance on the New Faces Show at the Country Radio Seminar. Music history was about to be made.

Their RCA debut single, "Tennessee River" shot to No. One, a place that became the band's home throughout most of that decade. They also began their succession of awards, including six time winners of the

They can boast of album sales over 45 million, over 30 No. 1 singles, and 150 music awards including two Grammys, eight Entertainer of the Year awards, and the Artist of the Decade award.

Academy of Country Music's Vocal Group of the Year, three time Country Music Association Entertainer of the Year, and five time winner of this award from the Academy. Album after album reached platinum and multi-platinum status.

During the early 1980s, Alabama also launched country music's largest charity event, The June Jam, held in their hometown of Fort Payne. Over the past eleven years, the event has raised three million dollars, drawing 60,000 fans annually to the 40-acre field behind Fort Payne High School for a day of music featuring new comers, major names, and headliners Alabama, all of whom donate their time. Over a ten-day span, the event also features a V.I.P. Celebrity Softball Game,

Soccer Classic, Talent Search and many other fundraising activities.

With the release of *Pass It On Down* in 1990, Alabama began another crusade: Saving the environment. Without preaching, the song made clear the need of each individual to do their part to save the planet. Alabama's ecological awakening found them raising public awareness, picking up cans and papers, and promoting the importance of recycling—yet another cause for this socially conscious group. Their many contributions include St. Jude's Children's Hospital, hurricane victim relief, food banks—donating their time to work in soup kitchens as well, and the many local efforts assisted by The June Jam. Because of this, they

Alabama with friend and peer Richard Petty.

Photo by Jim McGuire

were recipients of the Country Radio Seminar's first Humanitarian Award. Most recently, their latest album, *Cheap Seats,* debuted at No. 2 on the Country Charts.

Most significantly, Alabama paved the way for the bands that have become so prominent in the 1990s. They were the first to offer fans marathon three-hour concerts, to spend endless hours after performances signing autographs inside the arena for *everyone* in the house, to mix rock and roll beats with country overtones and even incorporate covers of their favorite rock classics into their shows. Without Alabama to take such career risks and make them successful, it is likely that country music would not be where it is, nor sound the

way it does. We would not have seen mainstream respect and acceptance during a time when the genre was considered "uncool," nor would labels have opened themselves up so readily to the concept of bands as viable entities.

Never afraid to take chances, experiment, push the boundaries—and always remembering the fans who are responsible for their success—Alabama remains one of the strongest forces in country music, still charting hit singles, filling arenas, winning new fans with each album, and never losing touch with their down to earth roots.—*E.H.*

TRACY LAWRENCE
YOUNG GUN WITH AN OLD SPIRIT

"I have no desire to be a pop star; I won't stray from the format that made me successful."

Half an hour before headlining to a full house, Tracy Lawrence smiles and modestly admits, "It's been a pretty good year. I'm not complaining." This is quite an understatement from the 24-year-old who was named "Top New Male Artist" by *Billboard*'s "World Of Country Music." His debut, *Sticks And Stones,* yielded four chart-topping singles: the title track, "Somebody Paints The Wall," "Today's Lonely Fool" and "Runnin' Behind." Lawrence has been featured repeatedly in country publications, the first album is gold, and his follow-up album, *Alibis,* went platinum.

An obsessive workaholic and perfectionist, he concedes that, despite having carefully researched the music business before moving to Nashville, "There are a lot of things I could not have envisioned. There is no way of preparing yourself for this because it totally consumes your life and takes over your world, from your daily routine to every thought you have. Someone who has not been in the business could never understand it until they walk in the shoes of someone who has been there.

"I definitely felt pressure about my second record. We had a lot of powerful songs, but you never know how the public will perceive it. I have tried to be fairly consistent with the material, as the saying goes: 'If it's not broken, don't fix it.' I have no desire to be a pop star; I won't stray from the format that made me

A staunch traditionalist, Tracy refuses to have any of his songs remixed for dance versions.

81

Tracy felt a lot of pressure while making the record *Alibis,* but now that the record's gone platinum he can relax a little.

The second album was recorded with the same musicians as *Sticks And Stones,* with members of his own band, Little Elvis, tracking as well.

A songwriter as well as vocalist/guitarist, Lawrence is not so self-absorbed as to shut out Nashville's finest. The city is a songwriter's heaven, populated by the best, and Tracy has put them to good use on both of his albums. "The privilege of working with them has educated me in the craft," he explains. "I'm getting into that inner circle, definitely. It's not uncommon to find people you are comfortable with and stick with them for years. George Strait and Dean Dillon are an excellent example."

As country music becomes increasingly accepted by the mainstream, becomes the "hip" thing to listen to, and is unfortunately watered down at times by blatant marketing, Tracy Lawrence remains among the most pure and traditional. Remixes and "Bad Girl Dancers" are causing a threat, but he asserts, "Not to my music, they won't! I have no desire to be involved in any of that, the doo-wops and go-go girls. I'm very involved in my career, headstrong. I have a steady program and plan for the next ten years envisioned for myself as an artist, and I doubt I will be swayed.

"To retain integrity, first off, you must be true to yourself. Stick with it. Don't let the business influence you. Don't believe the press and hype because we're all here trying to get through life the same way. I feel I'm one of the happiest people because I'm able to do what I want and make a living at it. Anyone not willing to give back that joy to their fans is truly missing the boat and not getting full satisfaction from their life."

Lawrence has been blessed with healthy good looks, and more than once, the press has capitalized on his engaging charm and the justice he serves to snug-fitting Wranglers. However, a college background in business, advertising, and public relations has made him him wise to marketing schemes and the over-emphasis of image rather than craft. When fluff articles are passed his way, "I don't read them," he states. "As an intelligent business person, I know the bottom line: being able to sing is only a small piece of it. I can deal with marketing people well enough to get my point across. I don't want misrepresentation of myself or my organization. I'm very stubborn and demand a lot, but not more of others than of myself.

"That's mainly why I don't read most of that stuff. I see artists get caught up in it, and I don't want to lose

successful, and I hope that I am giving fans the quality they expect, and that I will also be able to draw new fans toward my music."

In selecting material, Lawrence says the first priority is to please himself, because "I have to be happy with the material and image projected for my career. I try not to get lyrically suggestive; ballads and heartbreak songs made me successful. Luckily, what works well is also what I like. I'm not into story songs, although many artists have done very well with them. I won't cut heavy rock and roll or mushy love songs. They don't intrigue me. I like straightforward, honky-tonk dance music that people can relate to from their own experiences, good and bad. Sometimes, they might not necessarily understand the lyrics personally, but they can have compassion about the subject."

Tracy Lawrence's success is particularly dramatic, since hours after he finished his debut record, he almost died as a result of gunshot-wounds he received in a hold-up.

focus of my career or the person. I want to remain the kid from Arkansas with big dreams, nose to the grindstone, and pushing the limits."

Lawrence is decidedly ahead of his years in wisdom and stability. "My mother tells me I have an old spirit," he says. "She's been saying that for years. I've pursued this since I was a very, very small child. It was never about glitz, glamour, and television. It was about wanting to play music, be the absolute best above and beyond what anyone thought I could be. The only thing I try to do is be better than the day before. Every show has to be tighter, management must stay on top of everything—I want it all and I want it right every day!

"This has caused problems with other bands. Because I pushed so hard and was so aggressive, even during the days of weekend gigs, I ran musicians off because I hated mistakes, wanted everything right. I won't say every day is like that, but there are nights I come off the stage and beat my head against the wall. We don't use a set list; we structure the show as we go, and it has taken this band a while to get used to that.

Sometimes I don't feel I did a show to suit the crowd and I'm frustrated until the next night when I can do better. The band says it was great, but it wasn't what it can be. I push myself too hard, but the key to success is you've got to demand the most from yourself. Then you don't have to make verbal demands. It starts with you. Look to me for guidance and if I have put the highest expectations on myself, everyone will follow. We all enjoy what we do and if someone makes a mistake, they beat themselves up and the next day, they don't do it again."

There was a time when Tracy shared unconditional love only with his bulldog, Truman. Then in September 1993 he married the former Frances Weatherford, of Farmington, New Mexico. "I came to a point where I wanted to settle down," he says. "I want a family, and I want to be able to give time to it. That means not spending 300 days a year on the road. I hope I will be able to manage my affairs well enough not to have to play bars because I have to but because I want to."

Another of his desires is to see country music drop its barriers and become racially and sexually unified. "I don't think it has opened up that much," he laments, "but I would love that. The mentality of the business has definitely changed, but the walls aren't that broken down yet. There are a lot of things some people still don't want to accept, but the new generation is changing

that. It's a slow process because a lot of people who are so deeply rooted in old-fashioned values still run things and it's not happening overnight. It will be a natural course for this generation as racism and those things decrease. People will think less about color and more about character."

He agrees that for someone so obsessed with career, it is often difficult to relate to anyone outside of work. "Even my own family—I remember calling my mama to say I'd signed a management contract and she told everyone, 'Tracy's got a record deal!' I smile and try to explain what I do the best I can, but no matter how involves someone is in business, this industry is unlike any in the world. It is very hard, even for professional people to understand it because of the way things are run. Nashville is much different from pop music. It is a world unto its own and that's why so many artists here are drawn to each other—because we can't talk about it with anyone else. You shut yourself off in a way. You're on the bus, with your band, it's very secluded and scary, but it's part of what you accept when you get into this business."—*E.H.*

JOHN ANDERSON
THE COMEBACK KING

They called John Anderson the comeback story of 1992, but to come back, one would have to go away, and Anderson never did. He has been consistently releasing records since 1978, charting in The Top Ten and Top Twenty, even scoring a few No. 1's. He changed labels a few times before finding a new home at RCA/BNA, where he recorded the phenomenal hit album, *Seminole Wind*, which was certified platinum—his first certification since *Wild And Blue* went gold ten years before. On the heels of *Seminole Wind*'s chain of hit singles, and the success of its follow-up, *Solid Ground*, Anderson is one of the few lucky artists who is experiencing long term stardom among old and new country fans.

Did the success of Seminole Wind increase the pressure on Solid Ground?

Anytime you have, in simple terms, "a hit," there is always a certain amount of challenge to try and follow it up. Indeed, we wanted to come up with something real good, and I think we did. A lot of it starts with material. Great songs are hard to find. Sometimes you get luckier and lately it seems that we've been real lucky to find and write great songs. That always helps. People who are getting in this business often ask for advice—I always encourage them to try to write their own material. I believe it is a big help; it helped immediately in my case. From that point, we go in the studio and after so many years, we're working with friends and players we've been with before. You see how it goes down and if it's going well, you don't have to worry. If there's trouble, it's time to start over. Lately, there have been no flaws and I owe a lot of that to my producer, James Stroud.

In the back of your mind, is there ever a "What if . . ." based on what happened ten years ago?

Sure, it goes on. At this point, I'm thankful for the hits we've had and I hope if there's another calm, it won't be anything we can't get through again. Usually you have a feeling when things start to get slow. I knew it was coming last time. In our own camp, things were falling apart: management, different things, record label deals. When things go wrong, it's impossible to have hits for very long. I had several Top Tens while things were actually pretty tough in our camp trying to get business together, everybody arguing which song would come out. Again, that's part of the reason for the slow spell. Had all those things not been changed, we would never have achieved the success of *Seminole Wind*. We now have a great management team and label. The music business is just that—two words, and no matter how great the music is, if the business isn't together, the music will never be allowed to happen.

Do you believe in fate, that things happened that way for a reason?

I think so, a lot of it. If not, I would be searching out people to blame. I'd have grudges. It was just a thing that was meant to be, as having a bit of a comeback was meant to be. Hopefully it won't be over until we're ready for it to slow down.

Almost forty chart hits—how do you compile a set list?

Actually, we just do pretty much our favorites at this point. We're going to change the show around real soon. As we speak, we're working in some songs from the opening album.

Much has been made of the environmental message in "Seminole Wind." Is this an issue of great concern to you?

Yes, indeed. It will always be. I'm an avid outdoorsman, fisherman and hunter. I've always loved animals and nature. "Seminole Wind" is a song that stemmed from a lot of experience outdoors, especially as a young man growing up. There are parts of Florida that will never be the same and they are locked into my memory. It's the same with other places where I spend time. A lot of songs come in different ways: many of my ideas are inspired by the outdoors.

Could you please balance "I hunt" with "I love animals?"

I've never been happy about the killing part, but I do know hunters at this point have made up the biggest part of people actually doing something to maintain wildlife habitat. I find myself among small groups of hunters who really do care, buy land and spend money so animals can flourish—without hunting those animals. I hunt what I enjoy eating—wild turkey, quail, and deer. Again, it's such a broad question. I've been on celebrity

John Anderson says that his love of the outdoors and animals is what inspired the environmental message in "Seminole Wind."

John Anderson has been releasing records and charting since 1978.

good for the business, the fact that all these young folks are in it. Worst thing—I can't cite a worst thing, but one of the sad things is, sometimes the business gets in the way of the music. That happens in every facet of music—always has and always will.

Was there ever a point in your career where you felt pulled in one direction based upon the public's expectations?

There has never been a pull and tug. We do our music and to me, it's just that way. I don't see one side of it as more rock and roll or more country than the other. "Swinging" is as country as "I Just Came Home To Count The Memories." It's just what we did. We've been very fortunate never really to be tagged about exactly what we did. That's why we can work with Tony Joe White, Mark Knopfler, and Bernie Taupin. We never put ourselves in a category we had to stay in, and fortunately we've had hits with a lot of different kinds of songs from rockabilly to ballads to mid-tempo. We've been real lucky.

I used to hear "Swingin" on top 40 radio as much as country. Today, everything is separated. Do you think we'll go back to mixed formats?

I hope so. I would like to hear more of that myself because I'm a big lover of all kinds of music, with country being my most favorite, of course! There are a lot of influences in everything today and that's great.

What are the differences between country fans from 1982 and now?

Actually, I don't see a big difference in John Anderson fans. They're having as big a time as ten years ago, if not bigger. My fans have proven to be loyal, and God bless those people. I'm very thankful to them and I always try to stress that. People have supported and been touched by our music through the years and in turn, that's what inspires us to make more and better music.

The meaning music had to you when you started playing: how has it changed, and how has it stayed the same?

Surprisingly, through all this time, I love it as much as I did as a youngster. I feel this is something I was supposed to do. I felt that way when I was ten—that I would be playing music somewhere. My parents had a lot to do with it. They were very supportive, always. I'm very fortunate to have a wonderful family. It gets down to fate, like you said, and what the Good Lord has planned for us. I'll always be indebted to my parents for their support and love through it all. I consider myself very lucky to be able to fall in love with something so young and love it so much through the years, and to have been able to make a good living at it. Only in America, huh?!!—*E.H.*

hunts where I was told animal activists were protesting across the road. I love the outdoors, and if I can write "Seminole Wind" and get people to think about ecology, then it must be a fair trade.

Are you a political person?

Not really. There are different things we get involved with every year, like St. Jude. Clean water is something I'm trying to get involved in. I'm not political, not these days. What's going on today can no longer be a deal where someone says, "Look what I've discovered." We all need to be involved. If somebody doesn't do something, I wonder what kind of water my two year old daughter will have to drink when she is 70. If things continue as they are and nothing happens, what kind of food will she have to eat? As much change as there has been in the last 100 years to resources, land, and water, you could just double that and see if you think there is enough to last. Personally, I don't.

According to your press kit, your sister turned you on to country music. Is that accurate?

It's kind of like that. I was ten years old at the time, and had a little band playing rock and roll. She was into good country and folk music, so somewhere around 1 or 15, I started listening to hard core country and at 16, I was a country boy! She still sings and writes; she wrote "Last Night I Laid Your Memory To Rest" on *Seminole Wind*.

What are the best and worst changes in country music?

The best thing is the growth; the involvement and amount of young people turned on to country has been phenomenal. It's something a lot of people tried to make happen for a long time. We cut records fifteen years ago hoping young people would enjoy country music and I'm glad to see it finally happening. People before and after me have done the same thing and it's

"There's a big difference between luck and diligence 'Cause I'll take luck any time it comes."

RICKY VAN SHELTON
BETWEEN HEAVEN AND HONKY-TONK

There's a duality of ideas in Ricky Van Shelton's music that began long before he chose music as a calling, and in fact has posed questions for many musicians before him. That is the contrast between the spirit and the body. For Ricky Van Shelton, the contrast shows in his predilection towards albums that feature both rockers and gospel.

Look at his album Backroads, for example. "I Am A Simple Man" and "Call Me Up" are straight up country with a rockabilly flare. But in "Rockin' Years," his duet with Dolly Parton, his spiritual roots again shine through and they grow brighter on "Keep It Between The Lines." In early 1992, he released a gospel album *Don't Overlook Salvation*. How that album came about is a story in itself. To hear him tell it, gospel music and honky-tonkin' have always been battling for his attention.

"I grew up on gospel music. I guess I've always been spiritual. I got into rock & roll and soul in the 60's. In the late 60's, I got into country music. I played a lot of

Photo by Chris Mackie

of things in life: Blind you to your problems, blind you to your friends problems. Nobody knew it, but I knew.

"Drinking alcohol is a bad thing. I know you hear in the news and a lot of the older folks think that this guy's on drugs or that girl's on drugs, but they may be sittin' there watching the news with a beer in their hand. Alcohol is the biggest drug of all."

When asked if religion played a role in his giving up drinking, Van Shelton responded without hesitation. "Oh, yes. I couldn't quit. Every time I turned around when I had some free time I wanted to drink a beer. I asked God to help me quit and he did. Took it away just like that. My eyes have opened up."

His sobriety caused him to reflect considerably and one of the things he chose to do was release a gospel album that he had recorded two years previously. He dedicated it to his parents.

"I did that for Mom and Daddy and it was a gift to them. That's the way it started out and it still is a gift to them. But after I did it, I was real pleased that I did, because it brought me back in touch with what I grew up with."

moose clubs, a lot of private parties, a lot of fish fries; I played living rooms and kitchens and front porches. I spent my whole life playing music. When I got out of school, I used to work all day and play all night, like a lot of musicians do. I guess that's the best training.

"I moved to Nashville in '85. If you want a piece of the action, you've got to go where the action is. That meant great sacrifices for me because I love home family and friends and I hated to leave all of 'em. But I did because I loved music so much. That was the turning point.

"Then when I got to Nashville, I made a lot of demo tapes. I asked a lot of questions and met as many people as I could and tried to figure who people were that I needed to get to and then how to get to 'em. That's what I spent all my time doing. I guess you could say I got lucky, but I don't know if you can consider it luck. These people didn't just show up in my face, I hunted 'em down. There's a big difference between luck and diligence. 'Cause I'll take luck any time it comes."

It was while Van Shelton was in Nashville, enjoying the fruits of his labor that he realized that drinking was becoming a problem for him. "It wasn't an obvious drinking problem. Like I never would drink before shows. The problem was a personal problem. When I got through playing, I would drink a lot when I was home. When I got through working, I would drink a lot. It never stopped me from working. Some people might say that's all right and I say you're foolin' yourself. You're telling yourself a big lie. It can blind you to a lot

Photo by Chris Mackie

88   Ricky Van Shelton's gospel record, *Don't Over-look Salvation,* was dedicated to his parents.

K.T. OSLIN

FROM '80S LADY TO AGING SEX BOMB

Among the handful of artists who transformed country music into universal music in the late 1980s, none was quite as provocative and profound as K.T. Oslin. Here was a single woman—a woman in her 40s—who had the insight to see and the daring to show that there was far more drama in the lives of modern women than country music had yet revealed.

With the release of *Greatest Hits: Songs From An Aging Sex Bomb,* Oslin made a triumphant return to the spotlight. (You're right: Oslin came up with the title herself.) In addition to containing such signature hits as " '80s Ladies," "I'll Always Come Back" and "Hold Me," the album features four new tracks—and some of the keenest observations you'll find outside a psychology seminar.

After writing, recording and touring steadily from 1987 onward, Oslin took off all of 1992 to mend her body and spirit. "I got tired, I got bored, and I got frustrated," she says. "I really did sort of go to

Photo by John Lee

Oslin likes to make sure that the sound of her recordings is one that can be naturally recreated live.

Unlike many of her peers, K.T. Oslin made the distinctively un-country town of New York her home for a number of years.

Zombieland. I've been in this business a long time, and I think it just kind of caught up with me."

The three-time Grammy-winner sounds thoroughly invigorated on the new album. Glen Ballard produced the additional cuts and an updated version of "New Way Home," from Oslin's *Love In A Small Town* collection. "Glen's a very musical fellow," Oslin says. "In trying to find a producer, I was looking less for a [services] provider than for someone who was truly musical—who did arrangements, who did string lines—and not just someone who would say, 'That sounds good.' Glen proved to be exactly right. I just loved working with him."

Oslin is conscious of being able to reproduce her records on stage. "But I also think all that extra stuff just gets in the way," she explains. "You need a lot of instruments and catchy little phrasing when you're not really saying very much. If you have a lot of lyric going on—which I usually do—then all that noodling gets in the way." K.T. went on to add that "I put songs together that I think deserve to be that way. I want

people to listen to my albums all the way through, as if they're tapes that you put on for long trips.

Oslin came up with the concept and title for "Feeding A Hungry Heart" while watching a discussion about weight control on Oprah Winfrey's show. "I watch all the weep-and-tell shows every day," Oslin admits. "I'm addicted to them."

"You Can't Do That" has an equally modern theme, discoursing as it does on the perils of sex (and food) and the death of spontaneity. Oslin penned this droll warning with Will Jennings. "I told him, 'You know—all our songs are about love. It just kind of works out that way. But at this age and in this day and time, I think we have to be a little more responsible as writers about what we're putting forth as being fun and hip and cool.' "

Revived and exuberant, Oslin is eager to return to the music scene. And she continues to take notes for new songs. "I'm always interested in digging into people's psyches to see what makes us tick," she confesses. "I'm infinitely interested in that."—*C.B.*

TRAVIS TRITT

BREAKIN' DOWN THE BARRIERS

Once pegged as "too rock for country" and "too country for rock," today he can do no wrong.

J ust like his colleagues Alan Jackson, Doug Stone, and Trisha Yearwood, award-winning singer/ songwriter Travis Tritt is a native Georgian. Hailing from Marietta, just outside of Atlanta, he has been writing songs since the age of fourteen, and gone on to record three platinum albums, *Country Club,* which yielded three Number One singles, *It's All About To Change,* .which volleyed him into major league status with diverse chart-topping songs like "Anymore" and the classic "Here's A Quarter (Call Someone Who Cares)," which he penned in ten minutes and never intended to play publicly, and his crossover classic, *T-R-O-U-B-L-E.*

As recipient in 1991 of the coveted Country Music Association Horizon Award, Travis Tritt is a fine example of industry respect and admiration. Such elevated status, however, did not come easy. His against-the-grain approach to songwriting and performance kept him in limbo position for some time, pegged as "too rock for country stations" and "too country for rock stations." Today, he can do no wrong in anyone's eyes.

"We're trying to break down the barriers between different kinds of music," he says. "I'm a firm believer that there's only two kinds of music: good and bad. I like

Travis Tritt describes his climb to the top as an "overnight success that took eight and a half years to happen."

Photo by Shaun Clark

to describe my music as a triangle. On one side is a folk influence from people like James Taylor, Larry Gatlin, and John Denver. On the second side is George Jones and Merle Haggard, that type of music. And then on the third side is The Allman Brothers and The Marshall Tucker Band. They're all balanced together, all a part of what I do." This stylistic merge comes through in his live performances—Tritt is known to play full-blown Southern rock one minute, then perform a lengthy acoustic set, each delivered with equal passion. This is what en abled him to bring a Lynyrd Skynyrd concert audience to their feet, and what is drawing packed houses on his current "No Hats" tour with colleague Marty Stuart, who wrote and performed co-lead vocals on "The Whiskey Ain't Workin'."

As his breakthrough album, Tritt says the title of *It's All About To Change* was prophetic and somewhat deliberate. "People have told me about the importance of a second album and of avoiding the sophomore jinx," he explains. "When we finished that album, we felt it was even stronger than the first one. So if that second album is about solidifying your career, it gives another meaning to the phrase, 'it's all about to change.' " Evidently, his premonitions were right on target. Travis Tritt is country's next superstar, and his upcoming third album (which he was recording at press time) is certain to thrust him onto that next career platform.

He describes his steady climb as "overnight success that took eight and a half years to happen." He started out as a soloist in the children's choir of his neighborhood church. When he was eight years old, he began teaching himself to play guitar. After his high school graduation, he went to work loading trucks in a local firm. He kept this job for four years, eventually being promoted to a managerial spot.

Despite a steady career and income, music was in his blood, and he left the firm to pursue a full-time life on stage. Initially, he gigged around the Atlanta area as a solo artist in clubs, later assembling a band that has only experienced one personnel change to date.

During the club days, Tritt came to the attention of a local representative from Warner Brothers Records, Danny Davenport. In the beginning, he was purely interested in Tritt's songwriting abilities, but after attending several of his performances, he recognized all-around talents in the artist. In Davenport's home studio, they began working on an album, a lengthy process of honing and fine-tuning. Two years later, the project was complete to their satisfaction, and Davenport presented the tapes to Warner Brothers. Tritt was signed to a singles deal, and shortly after, a full recording contract.

The search for management was equally fruitful. The label approached Ken Kragen, who was comfortable managing Kenny Rogers and a very selective, limited roster. The label believed enough in their new finding to convince Kragen to take a listen. Travis Tritt became the prestigious manager's first entry-level act in over twenty years. In November, 1989, the debut single, "Country Club," was released, followed by his first Number One, "Help Me Hold On." More hits were on the way: "I'm Gonna Be Somebody," "Put Some Drive In Your Country," and "Drift Off To Dream."

While Tritt's obvious influences are Southern Rock greats and country ground-breakers like Hank Williams Jr., he prides himself on having diverse musical tastes that include such unexpected names as Madonna and Dire Straits. "Don't knock it 'til you've tried it!" is his advice to anyone whose listening tastes are segregated to one particular genre. He prefers to broaden his musical horizons, and thus allow his own work to grow and experiment.

He is comfortable with the current pace of his career, and has his feet firmly planted on earth. Success has not given him an attitude, nor has it prompted him to stray from his roots. He welcomes his crossover acceptance, but is not courting it actively. Above all, he stresses, he is a country singer, and has no desire to be anything else. Travis Tritt has based his career upon honesty, integrity, and dedication. Those factors in themselves make him worthy of a long and prosperous career!—*E.H.*

Tritt prides himself on having diverse musical tastes that include such unexpected names as Madonna and Dire Straits.

Tritt's cross-over appeal is based on his diverse musical influences that go from hard rock to deep country.

Photo by Eddie Malluk